WESTERN STEAMIMAGE

1951-1962

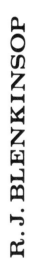

R. J. BLENKINSOP

Oxford Publishing Company

This edition published in the U.K. in 1984

Copyright © 1972, 1973, 1974, 1976, and 1984 Oxford Publishing Co.

ISBN 0-86093-297-4

Printed in Great Britain by:
Netherwood Dalton & Co. Ltd., Huddersfield, Yorks.

Published by:
Oxford Publishing Co.
Link House
West Street
POOLE, Dorset

PREFACE

It is now over ten years since my first book was published 'Shadows of the Great Western' and all four of the series have been out of print for some time. One of the reasons for producing them all in one volume is that within these pages is a record of one photographers work when steam was still supreme after the second world war. Also the pictures are in data order and as you look through the book you will be able to see how things have changed over the years.

Today, practically all railway enthusiasts carry a camera and produce pictures of better quality than shown here, but it was not the case thirty years ago. The 35 mm single lens reflex which is the norm today had not been born and most of us were on glassplates or roll film with its usual problems. I am sure it is prevalent in many aspects of life but I wish I could retake all these photographs on one of today's camera marvels where the chances of failure seems hardly to exist!

I still go out and photograph the modern motive power on BR and wonder at the technology of the HST — I will even change at Reading on the way to Paddington just for a ride. It is this comparison with the steam era and what is with us today that makes such a fascinating study and why we all look to nostalgia to see if today's scene is that much better.

My interest in railway photography is very much romantic in that I wish to be able to look at the pictures and get some feeling from them. For some it is the technical side of the locomotive, for others the record perhaps from a railway modelling point of view. For me it is the notebook as it were to be able to relive an event in my life from which I received much pleasure and stimulation. That is what photography is all about and why I went to such enormous trouble to take all these pictures, a labour of love when you consider the hundreds of hours waiting by the lineside and the frustrations of the British weather. That elusive sun did often shine but I cannot count the times when it was wanted and did not appear.

The pictures in this book are of course all taken after Nationalisation but apart from changes in livery and a few double chimneys it looks much the same as Great Western days. I suppose I should also include signalling, flat bottom track and the gentle intrusion of BR coaches.

But it must be the sheer variety of motive power in different colours which was so fascinating and to a certain extent one never knew the type of locomotive that was going to be hauling a particular train. You can visit the locations where most of these pictures were taken and still watch the trains go by, but of course there have been terrific changes, with lines being shut and the run-down of the main railway repair workshops.

For those of us who remember the steam era it is heartening that BR allow the various steam specials to run and I certainly look forward to the occasional trips which come through Leamington Spa.

I do hope you will enjoy browsing through the pages of this book and that it will bring back some of the memories which you probably had forgotten.

No. 7017 **G. J. Churchward** has just emerged from Whiteball Tunnel and

5070 **Sir Daniel Gooch** blackens the sky as it hauls the 13-coach 11.10 Paddington-Birkenhead up Hatton Bank on a dull day. The freight loop from Budbrooke to Hatton station is on the right and notice the telephone box for the banker to inform Hatton Signal box of its arrival. **12 January 1952**

The L.N.W.R. signals at Leamington Avenue station always dominated the skyline when taking photographs from the east end of the G.W.R. station. There No. 7218 2-8-2T sets off from the up goods loop with a coal train for Banbury. The signals at the end of the up platform are unusual as they control two lines. Normal G.W.R. practice is for each line to have its own signal post. **21 October 1951**

My photographic activities started just in time to see the last of the Star Class operating. No. 4021 **British Monarch** with elbow steam pipes, runs into Leamington with a Sunday semi-fast from Birmingham to Oxford. **21 October 1951**

Leamington and up trains were clearly audible climbing past Fosse Box sometime before rounding the curve at the start of the cutting. No. 6006 **King George I** in blue livery passes on the 11.35 Wolverhampton to Paddington. The first coach is a 1908 "Concertina" Brake third.
19 January 1952

The top end of Harbury cutting runs into Southern Road and Harbury Station and an up freight is passing the signal box behind 2-8-2T No. 7251. There is another freight in the up loop waiting to follow on its way south. Notice the typical Great Western signal box with blue brick base and metal chimney for the signalman's stove.
19 January 1952

The land near Harbury Cement works was often covered in cement dust blown out by the chimney in the picture. No. 6011 **King James I** is at the head of the 0900 Birmingham-Paddington. On cold days pictures were often marred by steam leaking from the inside cylinders of the 4-cylinder engines.
9 February 1952

"A" shop in Swindon works dull and cold on a winter Sunday morning. **North Star** can be seen on its plinth in the background with four Kings and one Castle in various stages of repair. Note the clean and orderly condition of the workshop—no bits and pieces lying about. The locomotive transverser would run across the picture in the foreground.

17 February 1952

Just two days after it hauled the funeral train of King George VI from Paddington to Windsor, No. 4082 **Windsor Castle** stands in Swindon Works with the Royal Coat of Arms hidden under a cover on the side of the smoke box.

The engine is in fact No. 7013 **Bristol Castle** which became **Windsor Castle** after changing over the name and number plates together with the brass plate on the cabside commemorating the visit of King George V to Swindon Works in 1924 when he drove the engine.

The reason for the name change was because the original **Windsor Castle** was awaiting a major overhaul and therefore not in acceptable condition. **17 February 1952**

Two pictures of No. 6004 **King George III** on the 11.35 Wolverhampton-Paddington. On the right near Bishops Itchington on 23 February 1952 and below in immaculate blue livery approaching the short tunnel in Harbury Cutting, on 22 March 1952.

awaits the return of passengers from Gloucester shed. Organised by the Midland area of the Stephenson Locomotive Society this was as usual a most interesting run calling at Gloucester, Swindon and Banbury. The engine is in black livery lined out in cream and red with red background to the nameplate. **15 June 1952**

Saint David climbs Sapperton Bank and into the tunnel at the summit. Next to the down line can be seen a banner repeater signal required on a falling gradient where with sharp curves a driver required advanced notice of the main signal further down the line. There is also a permanent way slack indicator standing on its own wooden tripod. **15 June 1952**

Outside Swindon running shed Ex-works No. 6026 **King John** produces the pungent smell much appreciated by the steam enthusiast. The cover for one of the boiler wash out plugs near the top of the firebox needs clamping in position. The fixings for securing the boiler to the frames, and, at the same time allowing for expansion, are clearly visible in front of the rear splasher. **15 June 1952**

Gloucester shed with 0-4-2T No. 1413, displaying its pre-nationalisation livery. Fitted for auto-coach working, the recessed footsteps are also shown to comply with the loading of gauge. **Saint David** is seen in the background.
15 June 1952

R.O.D. No. 3023 awaits its turn to be run in after a major overhaul. Always a difficult place for photographs in the afternoon as the sun shines from behind the engines. These 2-8-0's built at Gorton to Robinson design have such Swindon features as cab fittings, buffers, and numberplate with G.W.R. above the number, signifying that it was an absorbed engine.
15 June 1952

A study in power at rest No. 7034 **Ince Castle** having completed "Running In" awaits its return to Bristol (Bath Road) shed for top link work. A fire rake rests in the foreground and the shed chimneys are visible which were originally made from

Inside the stock shed at Swindon are a row of Midland and South Western Junction railway 2-4-0's Nos. 1334/5/6. The gas lighting in the roof above the chimney of 1335 shows the operating valve controlled by pulling the circular hook for "on" or the diamond hook for "off". **15 June 1952**

This is a general view outside Swindon shed and shows typical atmospheric pollution so much adored by lovers of the steam engine. Among engines on view are:—

No. 6828	**Trellech Grange**
No. 5016	**Montgomery Castle**
No. 6026	**King John**
No. 4062	**Malmesbury Abbey**

A variety of chimney shapes may be studied in this picture. **15 June 1952**

The Stephenson Locomotive Society ran a special train to Shipston on Stour behind M.S.W.J.R. 2-4-0 No. 1335 (Above) the train returns from Shipston on its way back to Moreton in Marsh and is shown crossing the Fosse Way. The four-way bull's eye lamp should be noted on the gate, informing both train and road user how the gates are set. Two red and two white lights are incorporated in the lamp. **31 August 1952**

Approaching Longdon Road on its way to Shipston. It was here that the Shipston branch left the original Stratford to Moreton tramway.
31 August 1952

0-6-0 PT No. 5408 has just crossed the now demolished Severn Bridge. Built in 1932 it was the first of the class to be withdrawn in 1956. The 5400 class had 5' 2" diameter wheels and were auto fitted, designed for light passenger work. Note the L.M.S. station nameboard and Midland fencing.
12 July 1952

The typical state of cleanliness achieved by Cardiff Canton shed on No. 5020 **Trematon Castle** as it runs along beside the Thames near Pangbourne. Note that even the top part of the copper chimney has been polished. "The Red Dragon" arrived in Paddington three hours after leaving Cardiff at 10.00.
5 July 1952

This is my reward for getting out of bed early on a chilly Autumn morning when the exhaust hangs in the brilliant low sunshine. 0-6-2T No. 6624 climbs out of Whitnash cutting with a freight for Banbury including an all steel cement wagon.

the signals at Oxford. The L.N.W.R. shed is in the background. Above the engine are backing signals with indicator boards and the engineman is crossing the bridge over "Duke's Cut" connecting the River Cherwell with the Thames. **4 October 1952**

No. 4943 **Marrington Hall** accelerates away from Hatton North Junction with a down freight.
11 October 1952

Steam shut off and the fireman peering round the side of the cab waiting to see the distant signal for Fosse Box, 2-8-0 No. 2814 rattles out of the short tunnel in Harbury Cutting. **8 March 1953**

Seen working a Birmingham-Oxford semi-fast, No. 4053 **Princess Alexandra** hurries by near Warwick power station with the driver seated in the usual rather uncomfortable position. The brass beading on the splashers of the Stars was removed during the first world war.
28 February 1953

It must happen by the law of averages that if you lean over a bridge enough times two trains will appear together. Here 2-6-2T No. 5152 is in charge of a Leamington-Birmingham local while No. 5185 assists a freight up the slow line on Hatton Bank.
28 February 1953

A view which I seldom bothered to photograph—the branch line train arriving at the main line station. In this case it is 0-4-2T No. 1444 at Cholsey and Moulsford coming in from Wallingford, with one of the later two Autocoaches. There is a wealth of material

freight passing through on the slow line behind 2-6-2T No. 6100. The first of the class built in 1931 for working the London suburban services and rarely used on goods turns, was also the first of the class to be withdrawn in 1958.
7 April 1953

A few hundred yards south of the station, the line runs into a deep chalk cutting crossed by a handsome brick bridge for the use of the local farmer. No 4053 **Princess Alexandra** comes up the grade with a London-Wolverhampton express via Oxford. **7 April 1953**

This is one of my favourite locations where the line is climbing out of Leamington and emerges from a cutting to run on an embankment all the way up to Harbury Cutting. No. 6013 **King Henry VIII** accelerates the 18.00 Birmingham-Paddington up the bank with a generous exhaust.
23 April 1953

Coming down through Harbury Cutting at speed in a typical early spring scene before the leaves are showing. No. 5055 **Earl of Eldon** has the morning Paddington-Birmingham via Oxford. This was a maddening train as on a number of occasions it passed as the 12.00 Birmingham-Paddington was coming the other way. For a near miss you can see the last coach disappearing on the down line of the earlier picture of No. 6004 taken on 22 March 1952.
22 March 1953

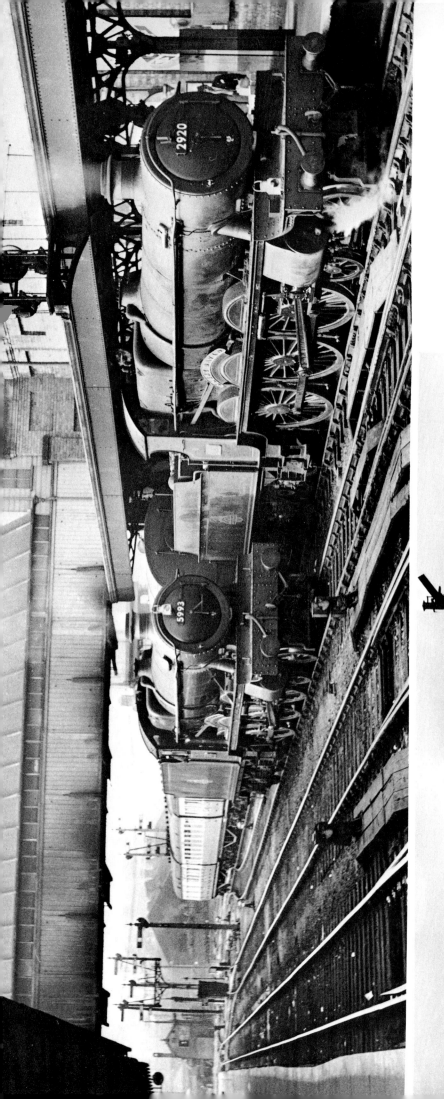

Shrub Hill station Worcester where No. 2920 **Saint David** has just uncoupled from a Hereford-Worcester train which after strengthening will go on to London behind No. 5993 **Kirby Hall**. Note the recess in the down platform to allow clearance when the scissor crossing is used. Direct design descent can be seen in comparing the Hall with the Saint. **6 June 1953**

Another Stephenson Locomotive Society outing to Swindon which took in the M.S.W.J.R. down to Andover and back via Basingstoke and Reading. Duke-dog **4-4-0** No. 9000 takes water at Cheltenham Landsdown while the passengers take fresh air and photographs. Note the stately glass awning over the platforms. **14 June 1953**

At Andover Q.I. 0-6-0 No. 33022 runs by with "The Lolly Man" chalked on the front of the smokebox. Mr. W. A. Camwell, who organised these specials and who is the Editor of the S.L.S. Journal, stands by the Buffer Beam of No. 9000. **14 June 1953**

0-6-0 Pannier tank No. 1991 of the 850 class and Taff Vale railway 0-6-2T No. 309 outside Swindon stock shed. A Dukedog can also be seen. On the pannier tank you will notice the square wheel spokes, buffer beam above the running plate, and the panelled splashers. **14 June 1953**

This makes an interesting study for the model maker and shows the 6-wheel bogie of W. 9001 standing in the down bay at Leamington after conveying American Railroad officials for a tour of the Shakespeare

The A.T.C. ramp is visible on the right and detonators are in position for the up fast in Leamington station. No. 6011 **King James I** awaits the

... of incoming stock make up the 10.15 Paddington-Wolverhampton as it leaves Leamington behind No. 5960 **Saint Edmund Hall** in polished black livery, a credit to the cleaners at Oxford shed. A G.W.R. railcar is in the bay and a wagon used for carrying aircraft propellers is on the left with the Avenue station behind. **19 September 1953**

On a foggy morning No. 1004 **County of Somerset** heads the "Cornishman" Wolverhampton-Penzance out of Gloucester Eastgate station. Un-rebuilt Patriot No. 45509 **The Derbyshire Yeomanry** waits with a train from Birmingham New Street to Bristol. **18 November 1953**

At Leamington with blower on and awaiting the "right away" No. 5032 **Usk Castle** has Hatton Bank ahead to climb with the 11.10 Paddington-Birkenhead. **16 November 1953**

the exhaust helps to make a live picture. No. 5027 **Farleigh Castle** makes a fine sight with the 11.10 Paddington-Birkenhead as part of the fireman's efforts goes straight up the chimney. The leading coach is the only example of 70' top light brake third with 6-wheel bogies. Note that the track was about to be relayed and on the left is a fogman's hut. **28 November 1953**

Wrong line working on a Sunday morning with 0-6-2T No. 6697 (now preserved) in the foreground and No. 6879 **Overton Grange** passing on a freight to Birmingham. The location is between Warwick and Leamington where the line is crossed by the Grand Union Canal seen in the background with another 0-6-2T underneath. **14 February 1954**

2-6-2T No. 5185 hurries down Hatton Bank with a local from Birmingham to Leamington. **7 March 1954**

A well built example of a 2-6-2T No. 6130 picks up speed after the Shrivenham stop with a Reading-Swindon train. **6 March 1954**

Perhaps not looking as clean as it does today but nevertheless a credit to the cleaners at Stafford Road shed, No. 4079 **Pendennis Castle** climbs out of Leamington with the up "Inter-City". The early pattern of

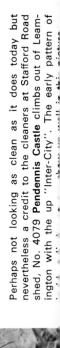

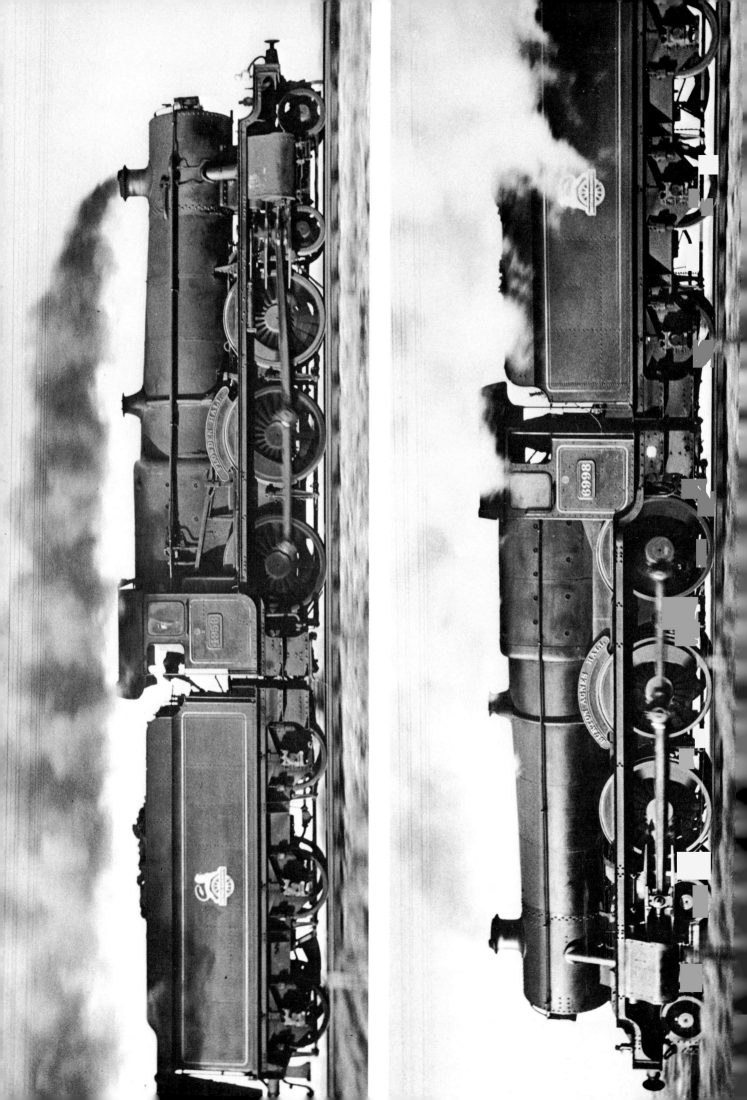

Halls at Speed
No. 4956 **Plowden Hall** with an up train and No. 6998 **Burton Agnes Hall** (now preserved) forging westwards into the evening sun, both taken from the same spot two miles east of Didcot. In the top photograph the fireman can be seen hard at work and the water scoop is prominent under the tender.
19 April 1954

Cup Final Day sometimes produced a succession of football specials to Wembley depending on who were the lucky participants. No doubt soccer enthusiasts can work out which supporters were being hauled by No. 6862 **Derwent Grange** as it comes up the divided main line near Saunderton with a special from Birmingham to Wembley. The cheery crew must have spotted me some way away as the driver has come over to the fireman's side of the engine.
1 May 1954

background whenever No. 6000 **King George V** came into sight at the end of Whitnash cutting. Here it is working the 18.00 Birmingham-Paddington.
19 July 1954

0-4-2T No. 1402 propels 70' Auto-coach No. W206 into Honeybourne station from the Cheltenham line. The coach is gas lit with the gas pipes on top of the roof. Originally it was railmotor No. 86 but converted in 1933.
7 August 1954

Under a stormy sky No. 6009 **King Charles II** approaches Hatton station with the 15.00 Birmingham-Paddington express. The Grand Union Canal is seen above the hedge on the right and the tracks to the left are for Stratford-upon-Avon and the south west.
11 August 1954

"Cambrian Coast Express" out of Shrewsbury station with another load of holidaymakers. Note the automatic train control pick-up under the buffer beam and the two platelayers in earnest conversation standing in the middle of the down main line having left their hammer beside the track.
12 August 1954

My first visit to "Glorious Devon" was damp to say the least but when sights such as this came into view it did not matter too much. Approaching Aller Junction with a train to Plymouth is No. 7815 **Fritwell Manor** with 2-6-2T No. 5150 on the inside. In the background a local train approaches for the Torquay line.
21 August 1954

2-6-2T No. 4179 at Aller Junction is on the down line for Torquay and No. 5024 **Carew Castle** comes off the branch with a Kingswear-Wolverhampton train. The rivets on the side of the tank engine's bunker clearly show the space allocated to coal and water. **21 August 1954**

Cowley Bridge Junction looking north with the Southern line from Barnstable coming in on the left. 2-8-0 No. 3838 approaches Exeter and according to the signals is about to cross over the main line. Note the long check rails and point rodding outside the signal box where under the steps can be seen a goodly store of locomotive coal for the signalman's stove. **22 August 1954**

2-6-0 No. 6398 pulls away from Tiverton Junction with an evening local train from Taunton to Exeter. The branch to Hemyock leaves beyond the station and disappears through the trees above the goods yard. There is plenty to interest the railway modeller in this picture.
23 August 1954

No. 6018 **King Henry VI** bursts out of the tunnel at the start of the promenade at Dawlish with the 08.30 Plymouth-Paddington. The leading coach is "Centenary Stock" built in 1935 to mark the centenary of the G.W.R. A sighting board helps the engineman on the down line to read the signal arm against the distracting background.
25 August 1954

At the other end of the tunnel shown on the preceding page, No. 4942 **Maindy Hall** emerges with a local train from Exeter, and 2-8-0 No. 2845 has the up line. The seashore beach huts are visible on the right of the picture. **25 August 1954**

A seven coach train with a history of coaching stock. The second vehicle is a dining car made in 1930 followed by a "Concertina" built in 1918. The leading vehicle was made in 1940 and the train ascends Honeybourne Bank up to Chipping Campden tunnel behind No. 7005 **Sir Lamphey Castle** (later named **Sir Edward Elgar**) with a Worcester-Paddington express. This picture conveys the feelings mentioned in the preface. **27 August 1954**

A County 4-6-0 at speed with the through train from Margate to Birkenhead and about to go under the S.M.J.R. near Fenny Compton. No. 1024 **County of Pembroke** is in charge with a bow-ended third behind the tender and Collet 7' 0" bogies.
18 December 1954

Depulising for the usual King, No. 5088 "Llanthony Abbey" has just passed Hatton station with the midday express from Birmingham to Paddington.
18 January 1955

Another view of the same train half way down Hatton Bank this time with No. 6020 **King Henry IV** in charge.
19 January 1955

ton Bank with a down freight for the Black Country. Beyond the snow covered field is the maintenance workshop of the Grand Union Canal and in the distance can be seen the smoking chimney of Hatton Hospital.
19 January 1955

The old London-Birmingham line of the G.W.R. is shown in the foreground as 2-6-2T No. 6102 takes the auto train up the bank towards Ardley and Bicester. The girder bridge shadowed at the top of the picture carries the down line over the old route and forms the Aynho flyover.
18 December 1954

Two moguls meet by the S.M.J.R. over-bridge between Banbury and Leamington. No. 9314 with window cab is on the down line and No. 6321 comes into view from under the bridge. Both engines appear to have steam to spare.
18 December 1954

Saint class No. 2925 in 1924 but with 6′ 0″ coupled wheels. The local train from Leamington to Worcester via Stratford-on-Avon is passing the cold storage plant near Warwick and the signal box was a World War II building. The mile post gives the distance from Paddington via Oxford. **30 April 1955**

...roof, certainly needed on this wet day. The line to Stratford-on-Avon branches off to the right. This train was followed by "Coronation" class 4-6-2 No. 46327 **City of Bristol** on the 09.10 Paddington-Birkenhead undergoing trials on the Western Region. **27 April 1955**

R.O.D. No. 3038 toils up the loop past Budbrooke Box on Hatton Bank with a 2-6-2T pushing up at the rear. **30 April 1955**

In unlined black livery 2-6-2T No. 4112 has a local train from Birmingham to Leamington passing over Rowington troughs (usually known as "Lapworth" troughs). The water storage tank is on the right. **30 April 1955**

Still retaining its streamlined cab this was the King fitted with partial streamlining in 1935. The bullnose prevented reporting numbers being carried on the smokebox and No. 6014 **King Henry VII** carried these on top of the buffer beam. In this picture the 09.00 Birmingham-Paddington rounds the curve travelling very fast at the foot of Hatton Bank.

with a good showing of Hawkesworth stock No. 1024 **County of Pembroke** picks up water on "Lapworth" troughs with the Margate-Birkenhead through train. **30 April 1955**

Fruit vans from the Vale of Evesham are attached to this auto train shown heading towards Broadway shortly after leaving Honeybourne. The engine is 0-4-2T No. 1406 and you can see the Cotswold hills in the background. **7 May 1955**

Rounding the curve past Norton Junction station No. 5081 **Lockheed Hudson** is in charge of the midday train from Worcester to Paddington complete with 70' diner. The engine, one of twelve renamed after World War II aircraft in 1940-1, is in a state of cleanliness typical of the Castles at Worcester shed. **7 May 1955**

A blast of steam from the whistle announces the approach of the evening Worcester–Paddington train to Evesham station. To the left can be seen the shed and Midland line bearing off to Ashchurch.

7 May 1955

No. 7029 **Clun Castle** nears Honeybourne Junction and is about to pass under the Worcester–Paddington main line with a West Country returning holiday express to Wolverhampton. Shedded at Newton Abbot the engine will probably return the next day on the Sunday "Cornishman". Note the fine G.W.R. signals with long arms erected around the time of the First World War.

7 May 1955

The evening parcels train coasts down the bank a mile from Leamington. The down trains come into sight through the trees at the left edge of the picture and travel down the embankment just visible above the first coach. Chesterton Windmill now so beautifully restored can be seen on the skyline above the whistles

Is this not a unique combination of King and Star? Climbing Hatton Bank No. 6006 **King George I** and No. 4061 **Glastonbury Abbey** with the 14.10 Paddington-Birkenhead. This sight was expected as the Star worked the first part of the 09.00 Birmingham-Paddington in the morning and the King took the main train, thus there were two engines available for the return working.
18 June 1955

Instead of a "Stag Party" the evening before I was married the perfect form of relaxation was to sit by the line and watch the trains go by. In this case it is 2-6-0 No. 6376 with a local train from Chester to Birkenhead approaching Bromborough on a fine summer evening.
24 June 1955

Working the 17.10 Paddington-Wolverhampton, No. 6011 **King James I** with steam shut off approaches Leamington. The engine shedded at Wolverhampton Stafford Road worked up to London on the midday

… No. 3013 Kingswear Castle passes with the Inter-City'', at that time worked by a Wolverhampton engine.
2 September 1955

No. 7822 **Foxcote Manor** and 2-6-0 No. 6345 have just departed from Chester station with Midland Region stock and are about to cross over to the up slow line which will take them onto the Western at Saltney Junction. The mogul is fresh from overhaul at Swindon and note the L.N.W.R. signal box straddling the track.
3 September 1955

A vacuum fitted freight by-passes Chester station using the Northwest part of the triangle. 2-8-0 No. 3827 has come from Birkenhead and heads south to Shrewsbury.
3 September 1955

Two views of No. 4061 **Glastonbury Abbey** at Tyseley Shed the evening before working a Stephenson Locomotive Society special to Swindon. Note the heater for frost prevention underneath the water column and the arm with cranked elbow which was necessary on the introduction of the 4000 gallon tenders.
10 September 1955

Halls under repair at Swindon works. In the centre No. 6997 **Bryn-Ivor Hall**, and on the right showing its super heater elements is No. 5917 **Westminster Hall**. Various parts can be seen on the floor including blast pipe, cylinder covers and a chimney over on the left of the picture.
11 September 1955

The first double chimney King being towed out of Swindon shed by 2-6-2T No. 5536 for photographs to be taken, although ash dust appears to cover the rear coupled wheels. You will notice the grit being put on the rails to stop wheel spin on the tank engine which was in great difficulty. No. 6015 **King Richard III** also has a self-cleaning smokebox. **11 September 1955**

Outside Swindon works No. 6000 **King George V** stands cold after overhaul. This picture shows the ugly final form of single chimney which fortunately was only fitted to a few of the Kings.

11 September 1955

L.S.W.R. 4-4-0 No. 30304 Class T.9. has just arrived at Welshpool with the Talyllyn Railway Preservation Society Special from Paddington to Towyn. Dukedog No. 9027 awaits a shunting operation before helping

T.R.P.S. Special now with the Dukedog inside the T.9. leaves Welshpool station. Shrewsbury shed cleaned the T.9. and painted the buffers white. **24 September 1955**

No. 5010 **Restormel Castle** was one of the first Castles to be withdrawn apart from "rebuilds" from Stars which except for 4037 were scrapped earlier. This picture was taken about four years prior to this date showing it hurrying the Wolverhampton-Weymouth express past Hatton North signal box.
5 November 1955

Ex-works in black livery 2-8-0 No. 2841 comes through Leamington Spa on the down fast line with a freight for the north. The point rodding has wooden covers on its full length as many of the passenger trains had their wheels tapped at Leamington, and this enabled

No. 5090 **Neath Abbey** approaches Chipping Campden station with a late morning express from Worcester to Paddington. The wooden gantry on the left protects the telegraph wires from the power lines crossing the picture should they be brought down.   **3 April 1956**

Later in the afternoon with a strong north-west wind blowing, the exhaust from No. 5037 **Monmouth Castle** follows the engine as it climbs slowly up the bank to Chipping Campden tunnel with a train from Worcester to Paddington.   **3 April 1956**

Two months after fitting with the early straight sided double chimney, No. 6001 **King Edward VII** passes Warwick station with the 10.00 Birmingham-Paddington. This engine was the first double chimney King

Cup Final day must have had a Midland club playing at Wembley as No. 5912 **Queen's Hall** comes through Leamington on the up fast line with coloured ribbon between the lamps on the buffer beam. No. 6861 **Crynant Grange** stands in the up platform waiting to

Still with G.W.R. on the tender side eight years after nationalisation, 2-8-0 No. 2848 coasts towards Leamington with a down freight. The fireman concentrates on looking out for the down distant signal as the safety valves pour unwanted steam into the warm

2-6-2T No. 4124 has just left Parkgate station with a local train from West Kirby to Hooton. This part of the line now taken up is planted with shrubs and as a footpath is part of the "Wirral Way". **2 August 1956**

A toolbox for P.W. tools and a platelayer's hut stand on either side of the main line as No. 7034 **Ince Castle** comes up the grade towards Box Tunnel with the 08.20 Weston-super-Mare—Paddington express. A North Eastern coach leads the B.R. coaching stock on this dull August morning. **2 August 1956**

Shooting out of the west portal of Box Tunnel is No. 5093 Upton Castle
with the down "Bristolian".
3 August 1956

2-8-0 No. 2843 starts the descent from Whiteball Tunnel towards Exeter
with a freight. The banker can be seen standing beyond the bridge in the
background after helping the train from Taunton.
3 August 1956

On the final 1 in 37 of the climb to Dainton Tunnel, No. 1006 County of
Cornwall and No. 4091 Dudley Castle have steam to spare before the
equally precipitous descent the other side to Newton Abbot. Above the
cab of the Castle can be seen a mirror to enable the signalman to see the

Round the curve from Aller Junction comes No. 4077 **Chepstow Castle** with an express for Plymouth. The main road from Newton Abbot to Torquay runs along in front of the wood above the Torquay branch. 2-8-0 No. 2843 waits in the loop for a banker to come up behind for the slog up to Dainton Tunnel.

3 August 1956

The sighting board shows up the signal arm position of the up distant for Aller Junction in the background as No. 7813 **Freshford Manor** and No. 5918 **Walton Hall** lift their load up the early stages of Dainton towards Stoneycombe quarry. A rather restricted railway allotment is well cared for on the left of the picture.

4 August 1956

King George III following gently behind, but the roar of the exhaust from both engines proved otherwise. The Hall class engine would come off at Newton Abbot. **4 August 1956**

straight up to Dainton Tunnel with 09.20 St. Ives-Paddington.

4 August 1956

as seen on the right of the picture and the mirror previously mentioned shows up well above the seventh coach.
No. 6996 **Blackwell Hall** and No. 5967 **Bickmarsh Hall** have a holiday extra for the west.

4 August 1956

A fourteen coach load, composed mainly of Midland region stock, comprises the 07.30 Penzance-Liverpool about to pass under the A381 Newton Abbot-Totnes road on the climb up to Dainton Summit behind

With steam shut off, B.R. class 4 No. 75026 and No. 6026 **King John** descend the 1 in 65 of Rattery Bank with the 12.30 Newquay-Paddington. Note the spring loaded catch points on the down line adjacent to the King and the bird which has been disturbed by the train. **4 August 1956**

Skirting the outskirts of Plymouth, No. 6931 **Aldborough Hall** heads west with what I believe to be the Cornish Riviera Limited. The L.S.W.R. main line to Waterloo via Exeter is shown in the foreground guarded by a typical lattice girder signal. **5 August 1956**

At the foot of Hemerdon Bank
No. 7814 **Fringford Manor** and No. 7909 **Heveningham Hall** round the curve and into Plympton station at the start of Hemerdon Bank. The black dots in the sky are birds looking for some lift as they circle on a hot summer day.
5 August 1956

then wait for the 10.35 from Paddington, which was also King hauled, and the two would then double head the train onto Plymouth for a further engine change. This photograph shows No. 6025 **King Henry III** and No. 6019 **King Henry V** with the 10.35 Paddington–Penzance starting the climb to Wrangaton shortly after passing through Totnes. The headboard should of course have been removed.
4 August 1956

Half-way up Hemerdon Bank
No. 7820 **Dinmore Manor** and No. 5943 **Elmdon Hall** are hard at work with a holiday train for the North West. Both drivers appear relaxed and are enjoying having their photographs taken.   **6 August 1956**

Approaching the Summit of Hemerdon Bank
The outskirts of Plymouth may be seen above the top of the bridge as No. 5098 **Clifford Castle** and No. 6839 **Hewell Grange** come off the 1 in 75 final stages of the climb to Hemerdon siding with another holiday train for

of **Cornwall** has an excursion train for Goodrington Sands as it blackens the sky and shatters the peace of the woods on either side of the line. **6 August 1956**

This well known spot for picture taking is deserted early in the morning as the sun climbs into the clear sky, casting dense shadows against the cliff from the exhaust of 2-8-0 No. 3834 with an up freight passing through Teignmouth station. The two brick pillars of the bridge used to straddle the broad gauge tracks.
8 August 1956

A view well known in G.W.R. official publications looking east and taken from the road bridge crossing the estuary of the River Teign. No. 5992 **Horton Hall** has a down train on a scorching hot summer day when all the carriage windows are wide open and with the passengers hoping for the weather to continue like this for the next two weeks.
8 August 1956

along and, although this train could be heard down at Aller Junction, I did not load the shutter on the camera until the black smoke was visible over the trees. No. 6957 **Northcliffe Hall** and No. 6026 **King John** struggle up the 1 in 41 of Dainton Bank with a Paddington-Penzance express probably leaving London at 11.30. **8 August 1956**

Brakes hard on as the 12.30 Penzance to Kensington Milk train has just passed Stoneycombe Quarry and descends rapidly down Dainton to Aller Junction. No. 6000 **King George V** with slotted bogie frame leads No. 6869 **Resolven Grange** on their way to London, dropping off the gas tanks (at the rear of the train) at Swindon for refilling. **8 August 1956**

The 08.00 Plymouth-Crewe has just passed through Dawlish station with an immaculate No. 1017 **County of Hereford** returning to its home shed at Shrewsbury. The train carried through carriages to Liverpool and Glasgow. **9 August 1956**

The Great Western enthusiasts who proclaim the merits of their locomotives and say that they never produced dramatic smoke effects to show up any boiler design inefficiencies, may care to study these two photographs. No. 1015 **County of Gloucester** with ten coaches returns to Plymouth from Goodrington Sands with a day excursion. The location is the final few yards of the approach to Dainton Tunnel where the gradient is **1 in 44** and the train will be travelling at running pace. The smoke hangs in the cutting down below in the woods on a summer evening when there is a flat calm and the shadow creeps slowly up the field on the right.

8 August 1956

No. 6003 **King George III** speeds the Cornish Riviera Limited along the sea wall between Dawlish and Dawlish Warren with the up train. What a magnificent place it is to watch the trains go by as one wanders along the sea walk for a gentle stroll. The fireman is hard at work getting the fire ready for the climb to Whiteball beyond Exeter and the engine has the final form of a single chimney. **9 August 1956**

A view from the top of Langstone Rock looking south west with Dawlish in the background. No. 5028 Llantilio Castle has a 14-coach load of Great Western stock heading towards Exeter. **9 August 1956**

Dawlish Warren station with the 09.30 Paddington-Falmouth passing through behind No. 70016 Ariel and No. 5098 Clifford Castle. Whilst the fashion in clothes may not change very much look at the collection of ancient "air polluters" in the car park. **9 August 1956**

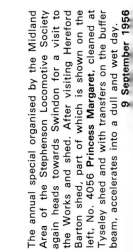

The annual special organised by the Midland Area of the Stephenson Locomotive Society again heads towards Swindon for a visit to the Works and shed. After visiting Hereford Barton shed, part of which is shown on the left, No. 4056 **Princess Margaret**, cleaned at Tyseley shed and with transfers on the buffer beam, accelerates into a dull and wet day.
9 September 1956

On the double track section of the Camorian main line, Wainwright class D. 4-4-0 No. 31075 and Dean Goods 0-6-0 No. 2538 have just passed through Newtown with the Talyllyn Railway Preservation Society Special from London to Towyn. The inspector and fireman appear to be having trouble in making the injector pick up. In the lower photograph the pair with their five coach load have crossed the Welsh hills and are on the descent to Machynlleth with a steady drizzle setting in. **22 September 1956**

Echoes of the

GREAT WESTERN

R. J. BLENKINSOP

Published by:
Oxford Publishing Co.
Link House
West Street
POOLE, Dorset

Printed in Great Britain by:
Netherwood Dalton & Co. Ltd., Huddersfield, Yorks.

1   This special train ran from Paddington to Stratford-upon-Avon, calling at Leamington for both engines to take on water. It was the first visit to the United Kingdom of the Russian Ballet dancers, starting a succession of cultural exchanges. No. 5060 **Earl of Berkeley** and No. 5065 **Newport Castle** are between Leamington and Warwick. Notice the two types of 'Castle' chimney, the older type having an extra three inches on the central parallel part of the casting.

21 October 1956

the bank to Harbury with an up freight on a bright winter morning. I was standing on the buffer stop at the end of the down loop at Fosse Box as No. 6006 **King George I** swept by at over 80 m.p.h. with the 11.10 Paddington-Birkenhead express. This kind of situation so infrequently happens but calls for quick thinking and pressing the shutter release at the correct moment. Even with a shutter speed of 1/1000 second the tender is blurred.

29 December 1956

3   This picture was taken on a freezing winter morning with the sun almost head on. The 10.00 Birmingham-Paddington express approaches Leamington Spa G.W.R. shed and is about to pass over the Warwick and Napton Canal behind No. 5047 **Earl of Dartmouth**. Apart from the 'up main' which is off, the other two signals control entry into Leamington shed and carriage sidings. An illuminated speed restriction board gives warning of the speed allowed over the down fast and slow lines in Leamington Station.

2 March 1957

4 I always thought the 'Counties' were handsome looking engines particularly when viewed from the side. Having just passed Warwick Gas Works, and the fireman taking a rest, No. 1024 **County of Pembroke** attacks Hatton Bank with the Margate-Birkenhead 'through' train.
9 February 1957

5 Sunday engineering maintenance often produced interesting working. The morning Birmingham-Paddington train has just reversed over the down line at Fosse Box and starts away South to Banbury. No. 6001 **King Edward VII** is in charge and the driver has helped with a request smoke effect which hangs over 2-8-0 No. 3839 standing in the up loop, with a coal train. A 2-6-2T is in the down loop awaiting to go on to Leamington.
3 March 1957

6 Running into Paddington, a 'Brittania' Pacific No. 70026 **Polar Star** has completed its morning work with the 'Capitals United Express' from Cardiff. This was the engine involved in the derailment which occurred on 20 November 1955 at Milton near Didcot. One of the recommendations in the report was to improve the driver's visibility and this led to the removal of the handrails on the side of the smoke deflectors. One can clearly see the rectangular holes let into the smoke deflectors to provide access to the running plate so improving the driver's vision. Note the double-sided water column and shunter's cabin alas all now removed.
23 March 1957

7 For a short time the 'Cambrian Coast Express' was worked by locomotives of the 'County' class and here No. 1017 **County of Hereford** leaves Paddington with the train in Great Western livery. It was also unusual for the headboard to be missing on this train.
23 March 1957

8 0-6-0 Pannier Tank No. 9400 brings empty stock into Paddington Station. The train comprises an N.E.R. luggage van and a rake of standard Great Western suburban coaches. This engine now sits peacefully in Swindon Museum for all to remember.

9 Both engines shown here are of the 'Hall' class but No. 4993 **Dalton Hall** which leads is in black livery and No. 6939 **Calveley Hall** is in Great Western Green. The arrival time was around 11.30.

23 March 1957

10 This was always a difficult location to obtain a good photograph of the 'Cornish Riviera Limited' as the sun was non-existent behind the station buildings on the right. The train is shown leaving behind No. 6026 **King John**, at that time shedded at Plymouth Laira. The attraction of this photograph, is father showing son the marvels of steam and one wonders if he can remember it now he is grown up. Another 'King' moves empty stock in the background.

23 March 1957

11 A modified 'Hall' No. 7920 **Coney Hall** leaves Platform 1 with an express for Cheltenham. In front of the engine can be seen N.E.R. stock standing in the parcels bay.

12 A dull wet day marred this picture of the first annual special train from Paddington to the Festiniog Railway Society Annual General Meeting at Portmadoc. However, No. 5040 **Stokesay Castle** was nicely turned out for this trip by the staff at Old Oak Common and a suitable headboard is attached to the smokebox. The location Hatton Bank.

30 March 1957

13 This is perhaps a rather orthodox picture of No. 6014 **King Henry VII** on the 09.00 Birmingham-Paddington, but I wished to include the splendid wooden home signal on the down line, outside the Harbury Cement Works.

6 April 1957

14 Signals and trackwork abound in this photograph of No. 1022 **County of Northampton** passing through Warwick with the Ramsgate-Birkenhead train, which ran throughout the year. In Warwick Station can be seen the 2-6-2T banker which stands on call for any train requiring help up Hatton Bank. The up signals hang down in typical Great Western fashion; it must be more than 45 degrees!

6 April 1957

15 2-8-0 No. 2851 is fresh from an overhaul but appears to have been cleaned at Tyseley before the day's work. With the regulator just open, it is slowly approaching Leamington with a down freight. The guard's van can be seen at the end of the cutting in the picture on the right as No. 6001 **King Edward VII** comes out of Leamington with the 15.00 Birmingham-Paddington express. Half an hour later No. 2851 takes the West loop for Stratford-upon-Avon at Hatton Station and passes 'Austerity' 2-8-0 No. 90238 held at the signals before joining the main line with an up freight.
6 April 1957

Built in 1950 well after nationalisation, No. 7919 **Runter Hall** is working very hard as it approaches Twyford with a down Worcester express. The modified 'Halls' were fitted with plate frames and these extend above the running plate.   **13 April 1957**

Firemen at work!

No. 6004 **King George** III nears the end of its journey with the 07.00 Plymouth-Paddington express. A smoke effect of this sort was unusual coming out of Sonning Cutting as by this time the fireman would be taking things easy.   **13 April 1957**

19 Beyond Reading West Station the up 'Cornish Riviera Limited' approaches slowly as the signals are against it for the road through Reading General Station. No. 6025 **King Henry III** has come up from Plymouth, and the other two photographers are furiously winding on the film to take photographs as the train goes away.

13 April 1957

winter a day like this is a real tonic, although the crew on 2-6-2T No. 6113 (with a suburban train from Reading to London) do not appear to be taking advantage of the fresh air.

13 April 1957

One never obtains perfection in railway photography and this picture could well do without the telegraph pole emerging from the top feed casing on the boiler of No. 6010 **King Charles I**. However the majesty and power is well portrayed, as the driver snaps open the regulator just after passing Reading West Station with the 15.30 Paddington-Penzance and starts the climb up to Savernake. The kitchen car leading the train would come off at Newton Abbot.

13 April 1957

One of the most interesting excursions undertaken by No. 3440 **City of Truro** was the 'Daffodil Express' organised by Ian Allan. 'Castle' hauled from Paddington to Gloucester, 2-6-0 No. 4358 and **City of Truro** took the train on through the Welsh Valleys to Newport. Both engines are shown being prepared at Gloucester shed with the shed staff wearing the usual cycle clips to stop dust and dirt from getting up their trouser legs!

18 May 1957

23 The train emerges from a tunnel near Mitcheldean Road Station on the single line some 5 miles from Ross-on-Wye. If only these pictures could be in colour you would see clearly the magnificent paintwork and lining on **City of Truro** together with the intricate G.W.R. scroll on the tender. **18 May 1957**

painted and lined out in green livery.

18 May 1957

24 A view looking West on the side of the valley near Pontypool showing a motley collection of goods wagons with wooden sides. An Auto-train is on its way down to Newport and a 66XX class 0-6-2T shunts in the yard.

18 May 1957

25 0-4-2T No. 1455 stands at Monmouth (Troy) waiting to leave with an Auto-train for Ross-on-Wye. Note the stone station building and the primitive water column. Beyond the short tunnel, the line used to go to Raglan and Usk to join the main Hereford-Newport line at Little Mill Junction.

18 May 1957

26 When the 'Daffodil Express' arrived at Crumlin Viaduct, due to weight restrictions **City of Truro** ran forward light (see left) and No. 4358 (above) comes into Crumlin Station with the train. After joining together again the train leaves for Neath (below). Crumlin Viaduct (now demolished) was built to carry double track at a height of 200 ft. across the valley and at a cost of £62,000. It was opened on 1 June 1857.
18 May 1957

27 Two miles south of Newport 2-8-0T No. 5215 has a mixed freight of scrap metal and oil wagons. In the distance can be seen the Newport Transporter Bridge across the River Usk and a ship in the docks.
18 May 1957

28 An up freight train behind 2-8-0T No. 4203 at the same location is seen on the relief line, with a train of oil wagons. This engine was built in 1912 and withdrawn in 1961. Note this early engine in the 42XX class had inside steam pipes. The 'barrier wagons' separating the engine and guards van from the train were to avoid fire risk when petrol was being carried.
18 May 1957

29 On the skyline can be seen the hills beyond the south coast of the Bristol Channel, as the 'Daffodil Express' gleaming in the low evening sunshine, approaches Newport for a further engine change. No. 4090 **Dorchester Castle**, (the second 'Castle' to receive a double chimney) took the train on to Paddington, during which a speed of 94 m.p.h. was achieved.

30 No. 6014 **King Henry VII** rounds the curve just to the south of Tyseley Station with the 09.00 Birmingham-Paddington express. The North Warwick line from Stratford-upon-Avon to Birmingham can be seen coming in from the left of the picture and the two relief lines have now been removed.
22 May 1957

31 The standard heavy goods engines of the G.W.R. and L.N.W.R. are shown here with 2-8-0 No. 3811 on the left. An 0-8-0 No. 49417 comes through Leamington with a brick train from Whittlesey to Worcester having just used the connecting line at Leamington Spa South Junction signal box. In my boyhood days the sound of these engines with their Joy's valve gear ascending the bank at night betwen Leamington and Kenilworth, was music to the ears. No. 49417 was built at Crewe in 1921 as a member of the L.N. W.R. 'G.2' class, the last development of the 0-8-0 goods engine first built by Webb in 1892.
1 June 1957

32 This picture emphasises the 30 inch stroke of the 'Hall' class with the crosshead just starting its forward travel down the long crosshead guides. No. 4954 **Plaish Hall** is half way up Hatton Bank and the fireman's shovel is loaded, although it looks as if he may be at work with the pricker as this fire iron is leaning on one of the tool boxes.
25 May 1957

Two of a kind!

33   It is quite a coincidence that two trains with the same class of engine should pass each other within ten minutes of the same place in Sonning Cutting (Above) 2-6-2T No. 6129 is on its way to London while No. 6115 will shortly shut off steam for the Reading stop.

(Below) The driver of No. 4935 **Ketley Hall** screams a yell of delight as he heads for Paddington to pass No. 5932 **Haydon Hall** with a west-

34 2-8-0 No. 2801 stands outside Swindon Works with part of the foundry in the background. It was probably its last overhaul, as it was withdrawn at the end of the following year. Note the 'Shunters' gig' coupled to an ex-Taff Vale Railway 0-6-2T. The box on top of the 'Gig' contained a selection of ropes, sprags and re-railing ramps often required during shunting operations.

16 June 1957

35 In the present state of the railway relic market these chimneys are worth a fortune. An interesting exercise is guessing to which class of engine they belong. I think the chimney on the left is from a 'King' class.

16 June 1957

36 Outshopped with the final form of double chimney, No. 6017 **King Edward IV** awaits its first steaming the following day.
16 June 1957

37 There is quite a collection of bits and pieces here, from the fire irons to the railcar in the background. Perhaps the 4-wheel Dean brake 3rd and 40' passenger brake van should catch your eye instead of the engines. However 0-6-0PT No. 2134 is of interest, as under B.R. it was transferred to the Midland Region for work in Birkenhead Docks and was probably fitted with a bell. It was also the last of the '2021' class to be withdrawn a month before this photograph was taken.

16 June 1957

38 A special train returning from Swindon to Birmingham climbs Hatton Bank in the evening light. Unfortunately my camera was misbehaving and did not record correctly the magnificent smoke effect promised by the fireman during our conversation at Swindon.

11 June 1957

16 June 1957

39 Passing the L.N.W.R. signal box at Saltney Junction, No. 1008 **County of Cardigan** joins the North Wales main line for the run into Chester General Station with the Margate to Birkenhead train. The hills of Wales can be seen in the background and are in fact the Ruabon Mountains.

27 June 1957

40 At Brombourgh between Chester and Birkenhead, the lorries of D & H Williams Coal and Coke Merchants are loading up from wagons parked in the siding. A permanent way gang are at work on the track with a ballast train hauled by 2-6-0 No. 78057, standing beyond the signal box. On the down main No. 6841 **Marlas Grange** (running tender first) has a mixed freight for Birkenhead. Note the observation blisters on each side of the signal box.

24 June 1957

41 No. 7827 **Lydham Manor** (now being restored to former glory on the Dart Valley Railway), approaches Chester with the 12.45 Pwllheli to Chester express. A Southern Region luggage van leads the train. I wonder how many model railways portray the supporting wires for their tall signals as shown in this picture.

27 June 1957

42 Another picture taken in the cutting south of Chester beyond the river Dee. A train for Manchester, on the North Wales main line, leaves the picture on the left as 2-6-0 No. 6339 approaches Saltney Junction with a train for Shrewsbury. The engine is shedded at Croes Newydd and the clean appearance should be noted. Full lining out was introduced as late as February 1957 for this class of engine.

27 June 1957

43 Approaching the City walls of Chester, No. 4092 **Dunraven Castle** nears the end of its journey from Wolverhampton with the 14.10 Paddington-Birkenhead express. The fireman is washing down the coal in the tender and getting the footplate clean and tidy before the next call of duty.

27 June 1957

44 Modified 'Hall' No. 6961 **Stedham Hall** passes Fosse Box at speed with a Boy Scouts special from London to Sutton Coldfield. This was on the occasion of the Jubilee celebrations, attended by scouts from all over the world.

11 August 1957

45 Even the cat looks at the trains and, being a black one, it certainly brought me luck for the next few days in clean engines and sunshine. Passing the Promenade at Dawlish with the 13.20 Penzance-Paddington express No. 5066 **Sir Felix Pole** looks as if it had recently been through Swindon Works. Notice in those days most of the cars were painted black; an un-

46 Southern engines were used between Exeter and Plymouth on the Great Western, to keep their drivers in training should their own route through Okehampton be closed for any reason. 'West Country' Pacific No. 34001 **Exeter** leaves Dawlish with the 17.45 Exeter-Plymouth stopping train. A 'Siphon G' ventilated milk van is followed by a 'Siphon J' insulated milk van at the front of the train.
24 August 1957

47 It is interesting to see how few people are looking at No. 7000 **Viscount Portal** pulling out of the station heading towards Newton Abbot. I like the Box Brownie user in characteristic pose taking the annual holiday snaps!
24 August 1957

side of the line as No. 5011 Tintagel Castle slows for the Dawlish stop, with a heavy load of 14 bogies.
25 August 1957

49 Kingswear Station can be picked out in the background as No. 6815 **Frilford Grange** passes Brittania Halt with a local train for Exeter. It is just starting the climb of 1 in 66 to Churston on the single line branch. The steam operated paddle car ferry was replaced by the present diesel model in 1960 and the two pieces of scrap metal in the water on the left are lying there today.
26 August 1957

50 Both these photographs are appropriate in view of the Torbay Steam Railway operation due to commence at the time of writing. 2-6-2T No. 5542 travels slowly down the branch with a British Rail built inspection saloon No. W 80976. The engine was one of a number fitted with automatic staff changing apparatus for working the Minehead and Barnstaple branches, but this was later removed.
26 August 1957

51 A general view of Laira shed (83D) taken from the road bridge carrying the A38 into Plymouth. The up train behind No. 5934 **Kneller Hall** comes down the 1 in 77 gradient with 8 coaches ready to tackle Hemerdon Bank unaided. On shed can be seen a variety of Great Western engines from 'Kings' down to '1361' class 0-6-0T.

28 August 1957

52 Dartmoor National Park begins beyond the main line, and this photograph taken from the A38 shows 'Battle of Britain' Pacific No. 34061 **73 Squadron** leaving Bittaford Halt on its way to Plymouth, with a train of very varied coaching stock.

28 August 1957

53

A magnificent sight with a set of chocolate and cream stock, the up 'Cornish Riviera Limited' crosses Blackford Viaduct behind No. 7813 **Freshford Manor** and No. 6021 **King Richard II.**

54 The carriage boards read Plymouth, Bristol, Shrewsbury and Manchester (London Road)' and the time is around 14.00 so the time table fan- atics can work out which train is being hauled by No. 5048 **Earl of Devon** as it approaches South Brent.
28 August 1957

55 No. 8451 was built by the Yorkshire Engine Company in 1949 and the sharper lip on the copper-capped chimney can be compared with those engines of the same class built at Swindon. Carrying a Newton Abbot shed plate, it is in a remarkable state of cleanliness as it passes Wrangaton Station heading towards Plymouth with a brake van.
28 August 1957

56 No. 6017 **King Edward IV** slows to 5 m.p.h. between South Brent and Wrangaton for permanent way work being carried out on the down main line. The curved arch metal road bridge taking a country lane across the line should be of

57 For the Great Western enthusiast this picture has a wealth of detail from the buildings, signalling and station layout. The name board 'South Brent (change for the Kingsbridge Branch)' is seen on the left platform complete with palm trees, and 4077 **Chepstow Castle** is coming through with the up 'Royal Duchy'. As a child I often wondered why the passenger footbridge should be fitted with frosted glass!

28 August 1957

58 2-6-2T No. 5533 comes into Brent Station with the branch train from Kingsbridge. The main line to Totnes disappears round the corner hugging the south edge of Dartmoor.

28 August 1957

59 Climbing the 1 in 46 bank between Totnes and Tigley Box, an unidentified train from Paddington to Plymouth has two 'Castles' in charge, No. 5064 **Bishops Castle** and No. 7022 **Hereford Castle**. The 107 reporting number covered the 07.30 Paddington-Paignton express so probably **Bishops Castle** came on at Newton Abbot.

28 August 1957

County of Middlesex drop into Totnes with a Royal Mail Coach leading. The Post Office Mail pick-up apparatus can be seen beside the sixth coach. The 'County' still retains the original shape of double chimney with which it was built.

28 August 1957

61 These three photographs were taken at the top of Dainton Bank where the main line disappears into a short tunnel. 2-8-0 No. 2875 is working very hard with a down freight. Note the engine is blowing off and 2-6-2T No. 5196 acting as banker, has already shut off steam before the tunnel mouth is reached. The cheerful guard will shortly be jumping into action pinning down brakes before the descent to Totnes the other side of the tunnel.

28 August 1957

62 A general view of Newton Abbot Station in the evening, with 2-6-0 No. 6385 leaving for Torquay. This engine, together with No. 6372 (fully lined out in green and polished safety valve covers) was used for working the Royal Train on 8 May 1956 from Taunton to Barnstaple. Note the locomotive weather cock beyond the shed water tank depicting a broad gauge engine.

28 August 1957

63 After working the down 'Torbay Express' from Paddington, No. 5008 **Raglan Castle** returns to Newton Abbot shed with a freight train from Kingswear.

28 August 1957

64 I have included this picture taken at the well known sea wall beyond Teignmouth Station as it portrays all the feelings of a hot summer day. No. 5028 **Llantilio Castle** is in charge of the 07.30 Penzance to Crewe express.

29 August 1957

In charge of the up 'Royal Duchy' at the end of the summer in 1957, as there were only 8 engines not rebuilt with double chimney. I like this picture as there is no headboard or reporting numbers and the level angle shows off the pleasing lines of No. 6029 **King Edward VIII** followed by an immaculate rake of chocolate and cream stock.

29 August 1957

66 2-8-0 No. 3853 shedded at Severn Tunnel Junction and sporting a clean black livery, joins the River Teign for its journey up to Newton Abbot with a short freight train. It is almost high tide and you can see the bridge carrying the road from Teignmouth to Shaldon in the background with Teignmouth docks beyond.

29 August 1957

ton Abbot and No. 6002 **King William IV** shutting off steam for the curves through Teignmouth with the 'Up Limited'. Note the milepost just about to disappear from view behind the engine.

29 August 1957

68   Perhaps a rather distracting background, but I liked the sweep of the stone embankment and the splendid old wooden barge which I believe was a primitive drilling rig for checking the river bed. The driver of No. 6008 **King James II** has just opened the regulator after passing through Teignmouth with the down 'Cornish Riviera Limited'.

29 August 1957

69 I covered 96,000 miles in the Morris Minor and sixteen years later it is still running around Coventry. Powderham Castle is across the fields to the left and the estuary of the River Exe behind the trees. No. 5054 **Earl of Ducie** comes round the curve with the down 'Royal Duchy'.
29 August 1957

70 Great Western glass lined milk tanks and gas cylinder wagons make up this lightweight train behind No. 7914 **Lleweni Hall** as it heads North near Starcross.
29 August 1957

71 No. 6017 **King Edward IV** approaches Parson's Tunnel signal box with the 07.30 Truro-Paddington express. I was to meet, at Shrewsbury later the following month, the enthusiast leaning out of the second carriage who evidently must have remembered my face or was it the large camera I carried?

29 August 1957

scene, it was taken on a brilliant sunny morning, with No. 4920 **Dumbleton Hall** (shedded at Taunton) making for the West past the signal box which is now sadly no longer with us. It must have been a pleasant occupation working that box in the summer or living in the house on the hill watching the trains go by.

30 August 1957

Express'. From the viewpoint near Dawlish the train can be seen further round the coast and by looking at the sky it is possible to calculate if a cloud will obscure the sun when the train arrives. A nasty black shadow creeps up the track and envelopes the rear coaches. Lucky on this occasion!!

30 August 1957

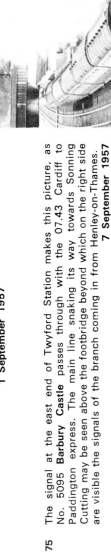

sion to Swindon Works and Sheds by the Midland Area of the Stephenson Locomotive Society returns to Birmingham Snow Hill behind No. 3440 **City of Truro**. Note the temporary shortened safety valve cover which was put on after an accident with the taller version.

1 September 1957

75   The signal at the east end of Twyford Station makes this picture, as No. 5095 **Barbury Castle** passes through with the 07.43 Cardiff to Paddington express. The main line snaking its way towards Sonning Cutting may be seen above the footbridge beyond which on the right side are visible the signals of the branch coming in from Henley-on-Thames.

7 September 1957

76   Twyford Station has a liberal collection of gas lamps and a strong west wind blows a mantle of steam forward from the safety valves of No. 4996 **Eden Hall** as it waits with a parcels train, on the up relief line. 'Brittania' Pacific No. 70022 **Tornado** is shedded at Cardiff Canton and left Newport at 08.20 arriving in Paddington at 10.50.

7 September 1957

77
Broadside view of No. 6003 King George IV speeding past Twyford signal box with the 09.30 Paddington-Plymouth express. The fireman is probably cleaning the footplate or adjusting the ashpan dampers.
7 September 1957

78
In the later years of steam the '4700' class were often pressed into service for the summer timetable. This picture shows No. 4700 with a West Country express bound for Paddington entering Sonning Cutting. This particular engine in fully lined out livery attended the Darlington Railway Centenary celebrations in 1925.
7 September 1957

79 No. 6000 **King George V** eases forward towards Reading West Station waiting for the signals to clear while working the 10.00 Newquay-Paddington express. The delay was caused by No. 30783 **Sir Gillemere** using the west triangle at Reading with a through train from the North to the South coast, changing engines at Oxford. It can be seen disappearing under the far roadbridge.

7 September 1957

80 After a turn round at Paddington of 3 hrs. 5 min. No. 70022 **Tornado** returns to South Wales with the 13.55 Paddington-Pembroke Dock seen here passing No. 5974 **Wallsworth Hall** in Sonning Cutting. **7 September 1957**

82 Shedded at Cardiff Canton No. 6939 **Calveley Hall** leaves Leamington on the climb up to Harbury with the Sunday 'Cornishman'.
8 September 1957

Weston-Super-Mare express. This was always a difficult and restricted place for picture taking, but this one has more than usual feeling of movement, emphasised by the low angle of the sun and a good smoke effect.

7 September 1957

83 Now with a tall safety valve cover reinstated, No. 3440 **City of Truro** approaches Shrewsbury with the Talyllyn Railway special train from Paddington to Towyn. The first coach is of interest being a 70 ft Tribog Compo with 1st, 2nd and 3rd class lavatories.
28 September 1957

84 Inspector Holland on the left with the Shedmaster at Shrewsbury stand in front of L & Y 2-4-2T No. 50781 which they prepared for the special. The engines are in the G.W.R. part of the shed complex, with an inspection pit in the foreground.
28 September 1957

85 The crews wave from the cabs as the train, now on its way from Shrewsbury to Towyn, has just passed the fixed distant signal guarding the approach to Abermule Station. The 'Dukedog' is No. 9021 somewhat obscured by the haze of smoke from the leading engine. What enormous springs the L & Y engine has compared with the Dukedog.
28 September 1957

86 Here is a level crossing gate guarding the Cambrian main line where it is crossed by the main road from Welshpool to Aberystwyth. Apart from the fixed distant signal that lovely cast right-angled supporting bracket above the hinges of the gate is worthy of study by modellers.

28 September 1957

87

No. 7828 **Odney Manor** takes the up 'Cambrian Coast Express' out of Caers Station on its way to London with an engine change at Shrewsbury. Note the Cambrian Railway signal with wooden arm.

28 September 1957

88

After leaving Moat Lane Junction both engines are working very hard on the climb to Talerddig summit, and in this picture are seen passing Pontdolgoch Station with the weather clouding over as the Welsh Hills are approached.

28 September 1957

89
On arriving at Towyn with rain in the hills, 0-6-0 No. 2239 shuts off steam for the station and is shown passing the wharf of the Talyllyn railway. **28 September 1957**

90
No. 7000 **Viscount Portal** heads the down Torbay Express between Slough and Taplow, and obscures a London bound coal train from South Wales. **5 October 1957**

91
No. 6005 **King George II** has just passed Seer Green Station and is on the falling gradient to Gerrards Cross. Probably travelling over 80 m.p.h., the train is the 10.00 Birmingham Snow Hill-Paddington express with a solitary Great Western coach travelling in style next to the tender. Note all the flies and dirt stuck on the front of the outside cylinder covers.
5 October 1957

All these three pictures were taken between Slough and Taplow. No. 4995 **Easton Hall** is on the down main line with a semi-fast for Reading.
5 October 1957

93

'The Red Dragon' hauled by 'Brittania' Pacific No. 70023 **Venus** makes for London. Perhaps the purist would disapprove of these engines being included but they were part of the scene and a very good one at that—handsome looking machines.
5 October 1957

94

There appears to be some trouble with the 'Hall' class engine as both the crew are looking over the side. A returning empty milk train headed by 2-6-0 No. 5398 is on the down relief line. Note the G.W. on the tender of the 'Hall'.
5 October 1957

concrete lamp posts and a winding mechanism for hauling up the Tilley lamps in the evening. No. 6020 **King Henry IV** climbs the **1** in 779 through Southam Road and Harbury Station with the 11.35 Wolverhampton-Paddington express.
14 October 1957

96 This appears to be an unusual situation as 'Stanier' 2-8-0 No. 48686 comes out of the sidings betwen the two stations at Leamington and heads a Nuneaton coal train for the South. No. 5070 **Sir Daniel Gooch** will have to wait at least ten minutes before the freight reaches Fosse Box Siding. Known as 'the Up Cheap' Wolverhampton-Paddington (via Oxford) it stopped in Leamington from 14.16 to 14.38, and originated from early days when few trains ran carrying 3rd class passengers and stopped at every station.
21 December 1957

97 This picture is full of material for the modeller and is a view taken from the cattle pens beside the down goods sidings at Leamington Spa. No. 6959 **Peating Hall** heads towards Birmingham with an early morning train, as the 0-6-0PT shunting in the exchange sidings takes on water. The Avenue Station signal box is visible behind the water column.
2 November 1957

98 The 09.10 Paddington-Birkenhead express nears the top of Hatton Bank behind No. 6009 **King Charles II**. The coaches include the standard cream and red livery, Great Western chocolate and cream, and the standard maroon shown on the seventh vehicle.

99 Further down the bank No. 7030 **Cranbrook Castle** heads the 'Cambrian Coast Express' on its way to Aberystwyth and Pwllheli. The down goods line and all signalling have now been removed.

2 November 1957

6001 **King Edward VII** as it passes Warwick Gas Works with the 11.10 Paddington-Birkenhead express. This photograph shows the bogie design with its inside and outside bearings for the wheels and the dished main frames.

21 December 1957

can clearly be seen as the driver gets away slowly to avoid snatching the couplings. Cleaning marks show up clearly on the tender.

2 November 1957

Road and Harbury Station, No. 5032 **Usk Castle** accelerates the 11.10 Paddington-Birkenhead express through Harbury Cutting and underneath a farmers road bridge which needs some drastic repairs carried out to the brickwork.

8 March 1958

...Maidenhead box and into the only ray of sunshine on that particular day as it heads for Paddington. There always seems to be a bicycle beside the steps leading up to signal boxes where the signalman can be seen at work.

1 March 1958

don. The location is between Maidenhead and Twyford.
1 March 1958

corner and, with a strong southerly gale blowing, 0-6-0PT No. 9429 is working a local train from Leamington to Stratford-upon-Avon and Worcester.

22 March 1958

The only days I could see the 'Bristolian' was during annual holidays or the Tuesday of the Easter and Whitsun holiday. This is the up train on the Easter Tuesday and is taken from the North end at Cholsey and Moulsford Station. Signal wires and point rodding abound in the late dusk with a colour light showing below the arm of the signal beyond the train. The exposure was 1/250 at f4 on HP3 film and the engine is No. 7015 **Carn Brea Castle.**

8 April 1958

107 A late afternoon picture at the entrance to Old Oak Common and looking towards Paddington. A 2-6-2T has a stopping train to Reading while a '9400' class 0-6-0PT approaches for the carriage sidings. A 'King' disappears up the flyover and a class 5 No. 45135 works tender first with a freight on the line from Willesden - Kensington Olympia and the Southern

108 2-6-2T No. 6103 makes for Reading with an evening commuter train as a set of empty stock are hauled up the flyover to reach the down side of the main line. A peculiar mixture of Gas Works, tombstones and car tyres dominate the background to the east of Old Oak

109 After a day's work coming up from Kingswear with the 'Torbay Express', No. 7004 **Eastnor Castle** has backed down from Paddington and awaits the signals for moving into Old Oak Common Shed. The Grand Union Canal runs along behind the brick wall and well

110 The 'Cathedrals Express' headed by No. 7007 **Great Western** passes by and, with the sun head on in the West, the spit and polish on the smoke-box glistens on this immaculate Worcester engine a few minutes after leaving Paddington.

111 Nearing the top of Gresford Bank, (a climb of 1 in 82½) No. 7800 **Torquay Manor** will soon be stopping at Wrexham General Station with a local train from Chester.

12 April 1958

112

0-6-0PT No. 5416 has shut off steam for the Ruabon stop with an Auto-train most likely stopping at all stations between Wrexham and Oswestry. The engine is painted green and fully lined out together with polished safety valve bonnet, and the signals are worthy of note. **26 April 1958**

113

This magnificent viaduct spans the Vale of Llangollen and the River Dee flows beneath. No. 5957 **Hutton Hall** with Southern stock is hauling the 09.20 Birkenhead to Bournemouth West express via Oxford and Reading West. **26 April 1958**

114

Originally built in 1932 as No. 9308, the 'Mogul' was renumbered as late as June the year before this picture was taken. These were the last of the G.W.R. Moguls' and were fitted with side window cabs, screw reverse and outside steam pipes. Note the tall safety valve bonnet.

At the junction with the Llangollen line south of Ruabon, No. 7330 has a steam breakdown crane in tow.

26 April 1958

115

Slowing down for the end of its journey from Paddington to Ruabon, No. 3440 **City of Truro** hauls an eight coach load of members of the Festiniog Railway Society. The sun shone and the 'City' positively glistens in the spring light, but alas the driver shut off steam just before the bridge. The first coach is a clean example of G.W. toplight brake 1st. The two coaches following are Craven built prototype first and second class open coaches and two prototype second class open vehicles built at Doncaster.

26 April 1958

116 After an engine change at Ruabon the F.R.S. special travels on to Minffordd via Corwen and Dolgellau. Both photographs were taken from the roadside of the A5 and show No. 9017 (now on the Bluebell line) and No. 9021 working on the single line. In the bottom picture the Llantysilio Mountains dominate the scene and the sun miraculously comes through to sparkle on the clear water of the River Dee. Inspector Holland con-

117 This could be classed as an interloper, but after all the 'Duke' did under-go test on the Western Region and this is the only time I saw it in clean condition. It is seen leaving Crewe with a 'Trains Illustrated' special. The dark sky is a torrential storm sweeping over Crewe and, as luck would have it, the sun was shining as the train came past Basford Hall Junction signal box on its way to Euston with the ex-'Devon Belle' observation

118 This is the first picture taken on my final visit to the West Country by car on a very dull day. An early start from home was necessary, to meet up with the down 'Bristolian' betwen Didcot and Steventon. No. 6015 **King Richard III** was travelling very fast on a rising gradient and for a moment the sun came through the clouds as the train swept by.

119 Driving on further south, I came to Newbury to see the down 'Cornish Riviera Express' come through the station behind No. 6004 **King George III**. 2-6-0 No. 7317 waits with a freight in the platform. Note the water

Reflections of the GREAT WESTERN

R. J. BLENKINSOP

Published by:
Oxford Publishing Co.
Link House
West Street
POOLE, Dorset

Printed in Great Britain by:
Netherwood Dalton & Co. Ltd., Huddersfield, Yorks.

1   While at Winchester I wished to obtain a picture of a Mogul leaving the Great Western Station, but due to the lack of light in the cutting I had to go into Bar End goods yard and photograph from the footbridge. No. 5326 will have started its journey from the down bay at Didcot and will come to the buffer stops in Southampton Terminus station after joining the Southern main line at Shawford Junction. Visit the scene today, and you will be amazed how a Railway could ever have run here. I well remember the **Collet** 0-6-0's which used to shunt in this yard and were known by the Winchester College boys as "Caesar" and "Pompei".

The last passenger train ran on 9 September 1961 and 2-6-4T No. 80082 worked the last freight from Bar End on 2 April 1966.

19 May 1958

2 After a photographic session at Winchester and Salisbury I had by the next day motored onto Yeovil, and this scene shows a Taunton to Yeovil Pen Mill train about to enter Pen Mill station just half a mile from Yeovil Town station. Plenty of interest here with the line to Weymouth at the left side of the picture, cattle pens, locomotive shed and interesting track work, including three slip points. Note the calling on signal above the first coach. No. 5548 is in the "lined out" green livery which was applied to many of the class from 1958 onwards.
20 May 1958

3 The sun shimmers on the sea as No. 6868 **Penrhos Grange** is about to enter Teignmouth station. In the distance can be seen the coastline around Exmouth and, as this is the off season, the sea wall walk is deserted.
21 May 1958

5 I then drove quickly to Newton Abbot and the Torquay branch just south of Aller junction beside an attractive orchard. The sun had not come round to light up the nearside of the train but with careful exposure the detail is rendered in the shadow areas. No. 7809 **Childrey Manor** takes an empty freight through a lovely summer setting on its way perhaps to Kingswear.
21 May 1958

as it was unusual to find two engines working the 08.00 Plymouth-Manchester with through coach to Glasgow. No. 6852 **Headbourne Grange** will probably work back to its home shed at Bristol while No. 5073 **Blenheim** will continue as far as Shrewsbury where a London Midland engine will take over. Notice the brilliant lighting often found at the seaside, a photographer's dream.
21 May 1958

7 After the up "Torbay Express" had gone there was just time to drive to the tunnel at Dainton to see the midday Plymouth-Paddington come up the last few yards of the steep gradient. No. 7814 **Fringford Manor** gives a helping hand to No. 7032 **Denbigh Castle** and yet again the sun shines.
21 May 1958

played for the sun to shine as the up "Torbay Express" shut off steam at the approach to Aller Junction. This is one of my favourite pictures with a beam of brilliant sun, back lit, smoke drifting over the coaches, a clean engine and a background of glorious Devon showing off the handsome lines of No. 5078 **Beaufort**. Note the fogman's hut with a side observation window.
21 May 1958

the Torquay branch and back again to Newton Abbot where it is shown shunting stock outside the station.

The road bridge carries the main Newton Abbot road to Torquay and you can see just in front of the buffer beam a device for signal wire tension compensation.

21 May 1958

...o 6 6 parallel tanks stand at the platform of Newton Abbot station as an immaculate Castle class engine No. 5074 **Hampden** comes through the station without stopping, on its way to Torquay. The track layout and signalling are worthy of study and also the wooden signal box with outside lavatory.

21 May 1958

10 The next three photographs were all taken from the west embankment just to the south of Newton Abbot station, and show a variety of train movement and stock. No. 6027 **King Richard I**, approaches slowly with the afternoon express from Plymouth to London. The second coach is an early dining car. **21 May 1958**

11 This picture shows the two large signal gantries guarding the approach from the South. With a Royal Mail coach leading, the train has No. 5056 **Earl of Powis** at its head, with No. 4970 **Sketty Hall** piloting (to be detached at Newton Abbot). The Royal Mail coach is a true Great Western product. **21 May 1958**

12 Plenty of activity here. After shunting stock No. 6868 **Penrhos Grange** finally sets out for Torquay with a local, and No. 7813 **Freshford Manor** waits to move forward into Newton Abbot shed. But, of course, the main interest is centred on the coaching stock behind No. 6029 **King Edward VIII** as it approaches slowly with an Ocean Liner Express from Plymouth to Paddington. The first two coaches are B.R. luggage vans followed by an immaculate set of "Centenary stock", not often seen as a complete rake after 1958.

13 Later, in the evening No. 5074 **Hampden** is shown at Aller Junction on its way back to Newton Abbot shed with a short freight from Kingswear.
21 May 1958

14 From the shadows in the grass one can see the sun is getting low in the sky, but it still provides a brilliant light for a busy scene near Aller Junction An unidentified "Hall" pilots No. 6993 **Arthog Hall** on the Penzance to Kensington Milk train.

On the down fast a freight approaches for Plymouth behind 2-8-0 No. 2843 with a 2-6-2T No. 5153 ready to help by pushing behind on the hard
21 May 1958

15 The last picture of the day shows a clean 2-6-2T No. 4117 approaching Aller Junction with a local train for Torquay and a set of late Great Western suburban stock. **21 May 1958**

16 During the night a warm front came in from the Atlantic and I was in for a day of wet weather. However, lack of sun should not deter the railway photographer as the scene takes on a different form of lighting. No. 6026 **King John** is half a mile from the summit of Dainton Bank, heading for London with the "Mayflower", including two Great Western dining cars. **22 May 1958**

17 Totnes Station, a scene full of interest, with No. 7017 **G. J. Churchward** entering with the 07.30 Truro-Paddington. Three 2-6-2T's are visible, two in the foreground and the third above the Great Western Restaurant Car (the fourth vehicle in the train).

Milk Tanks are visible in the yard and a Permanent Way gang

awaiting banking duty. This picture shows it hard at work giving a helping hand as a freight train starts the climb out of Totnes up Rattery Bank. Comparison with picture 60 in my previous book *Echoes of the Great Western* will show that the down main has now been relaid with flat bottom track. The gradient is 1 in 66 and the No. 2 target number shows up on the back of the tender. An I.C.I. wagon is visible together with an L.N.E.R. design "Queen Mary" brake van built by British Rail.

22 May 1958

19 No. 6808 **Beenham Grange** passes an Agricultural Distributor to the east of Ivybridge. The stone chimney would have been part of the original China Clay works built on this site, and the end of the line for the 3 ft. gauge Ivybridge China Clay Co.'s 6½ mile narrow gauge system up to Green Hill. Known locally as the Red Lake Tramway, it used two Kerr Stuart locomotives; the track was dismantled in 1933.

22 May 1958

20 Three-quarters of a mile further west the "Cornish Riviera Express", in driving rain has just come off the viaduct at Ivybridge, hauled by No. 4908 **Broome Hall** and No. 6024 **King Edward I**.

22 May 1958

22 I spent the night in Plymouth and hoped for better weather the next day. Sure enough, the sun was shining again as 0-6-0PT No. 9716 has a freight in the outskirts of Plymouth. The picture was taken from the A38 road just south of Laira shed. The track of the 4' 6" gauge Lee Moor Tramway may be seen ballast filled, for horse traction. Petrol tank wagons, and L.M.S. and G.W.R. Cattle wagons are visible.
23 May 1958

Although you can't see it, the poor old camera sheltering under an umbrella is about to take off in the wind! No. 5992 Horton Hall and No. 7032 Denbigh Castle, with an assortment of Great Western stock, are working hard in the up direction. The Royal Mail coach is the same one as in picture eleven but shows the side without the net.
22 May 1958

23 Storm clouds are building up over Dartmoor as No. 7916 **Mobberley Hall** runs alongside the River Plym estuary with a down stopping train for Plymouth North Road station. Note the double-sided catch point.
23 May 1958

24 An 0-6-0PT passes Laira Junction box and is about to cross the Lee Moor Tramway (still in use at this time by one horse hauled train per week). The wooden planks inset between the rails were to enable the horses to walk safely. On the extreme left can be seen one of the standard Great Western signals to protect the crossing. This famous main line crossing was finally removed in October 1960.
23 May 1958

25 Outside Laira shed stands No. 6026 **King John** being prepared for its journey to London, hauling the 12.05 from Plymouth North Road station. The wheel balance weights show prominently and also the enormous rear driving axle spring. Notice the haircuts of the cleaning gang, short by today's standards.
23 May 1958

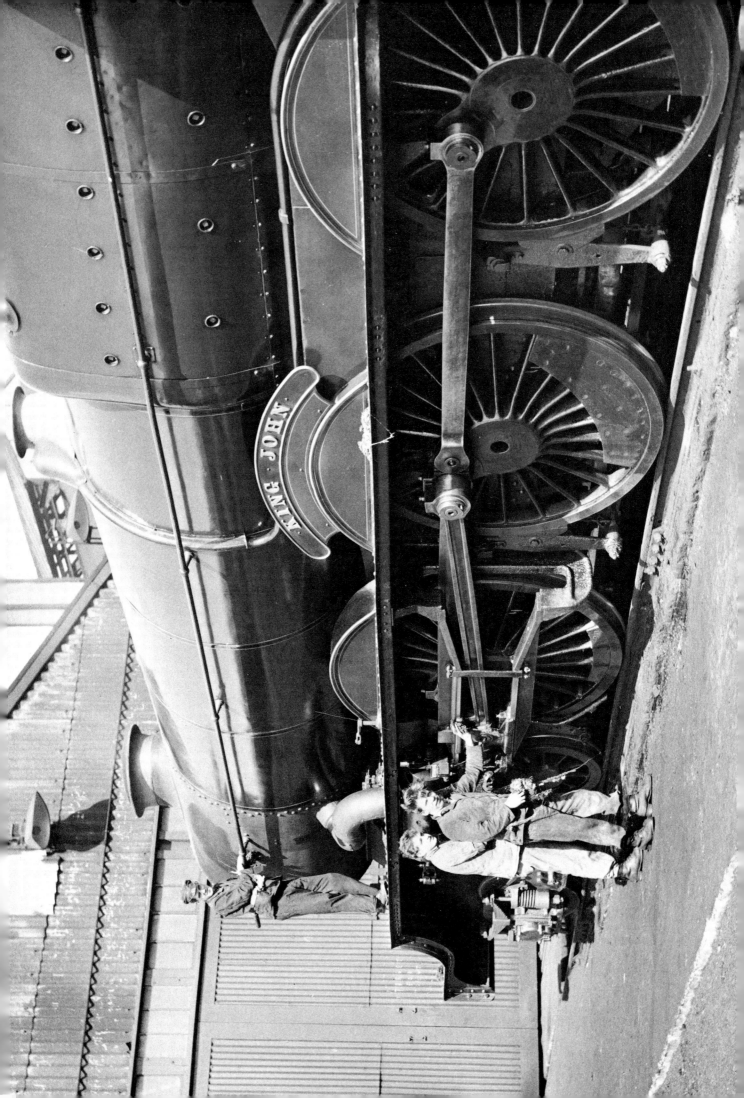

in 83 incline to Mutley Tunnel with the Southern line coming in from the left at Lipson Junction. Although both engines will be coasting, it is only No. 6800 **Arlington Grange** which shows life and this from a surplus of steam. No. 7909 **Heveningham Hall** is acting as a pilot for the gradients ahead to Newton Abbot. **23 May 1958**

27 Passing Laira shed with an Auto-train for Plymouth North Road Station, is 0-6-0PT No. 6406 and two trailer cars made especially for the Plymouth area. These were fitted with corridor connections, end loading and no centre doors. **23 May 1958**

28 This picture should not require a caption as it must be Laira shed and the most famous nameplate in the Great Western repertoire. The driver is probably oiling the inside motion. No. 7027 **Thornbury Castle** is immediately behind being prepared for the up "Royal Duchy". **23 May 1958**

29 Standing now at the south end of the Laira triangle we have a Battle of Britain Pacific No. 34062 **17 Squadron** starting the climb from Plymouth Friary, up to Plymouth North Road station and then on to London (via Exeter). No. 6911 **Holker Hall** is waiting to back up to North Road station following the passenger train and No. 6026 **King John** will then follow the Hall.
23 May 1958

30 After a morning of preparation and looking beautifully clean, No. 6004 **King George III** stands on the east side of Laira triangle waiting its turn to back up to North Road station.
The present diesel depot is off the picture to the right but you can see in the background a tool van and mess van for the breakdown train.
23 May 1958

31 having seen the two Kings off shed I drove up to the top of Hemerdon Bank to see them accelerating away from the summit. Just beyond the car the road passes under the railway and the bridge was being replaced necessitating a 5 m.p.h. P.W.S.

However, as the 12.05 p.m. Plymouth came along, the sun shone and the "Grange" provided a promised smoke effect, although both engines had steam shut off.

No. 6026 **King John** is being piloted by No. 6870 **Bodicote Grange.**

23 May 1958

32 This is the second photograph of No. 6004 **King George III** taken at Hemerdon and it shows the crew letting the engine almost come to a stand for a special picture of them on their "pride and joy". I had spent a good ten minutes at Laira polishing the front axle box cover so it would sparkle in the sun (the other side was not so clean!!) and you will notice the brass plate on the cab side giving the name of the driver and fireman.

The strong wind blows the smoke forward and into the trees.

23 May 1958

33 The sun has now gone in but there is plenty of light about as the next train passes the P.W.S. in an up direction.
No. 7814 **Fringford Manor** pilots No. 5054 **Earl of Ducie** with a Great Western corridor third built in 1948. **23 May 1958**

34 Nearing the end of its day's work with the down "Cornish Riviera Express", No. 6023 **King Edward II** has No. 4956 **Plowden Hall** as pilot as they accelerate away from Hemerdon Siding signal box and down the gradient to Plympton. **23 May 1958**

35 On the gradient profile two miles of 1 in 42 looks impressive and to see it at its best, the view from this overbridge looking down into Plymouth is splendid. Coming up the final 100 yards is 2-8-0 No. 3862, one of the last of its class built in November 1942, and judging by the state of its paintwork it is recently out of Swindon works.
The second wagon is a "Mica B" refrigerated meat van with access in the roof for filling with ice.

36 In picture thirty-five we saw the front end of an up freight, and here we see 2-6-2T No. 5148 pushing up at the back with a Great Western steam crane in front. This would always be marshalled next to the guard's van so the guard could keep his eye on it!
23 May 1958

37 I was now making my way back to Newton Abbot to stay the night but stopped in one of the lanes two miles north-east of Totnes to see a few trains start the climb up to Dainton.
   This first picture is of No. 6870 **Bodicote Grange** coming down towards Totnes with the sun being reflected off the boiler barrel and piston rod.
23 May 1958

38 In picture twenty-nine No. 6911 was last seen backing up to Plymouth North Road station.
   Here it is piloting No. 6028 **King George VI** in a very rural setting but not allowing the complete train to be included. The speed is around 45-

39 The next day was dull again so I did not start operations until it was up "Cornish Riviera" time. At least without sun one can take pictures from the side of the line which would be impossible if the sun was shining. Here is an example with No. 6003 **King George IV** being piloted by No. 6849 ... on the last few yards before Dainton Tunnel. The

40 Just to the north of Torre No. 7316 struggles up the 1 in 73 incline on its way to Newton Abbot from Torquay. This engine was built at Swindon Works in 1921 from parts supplied by Robert Stephenson & Co.

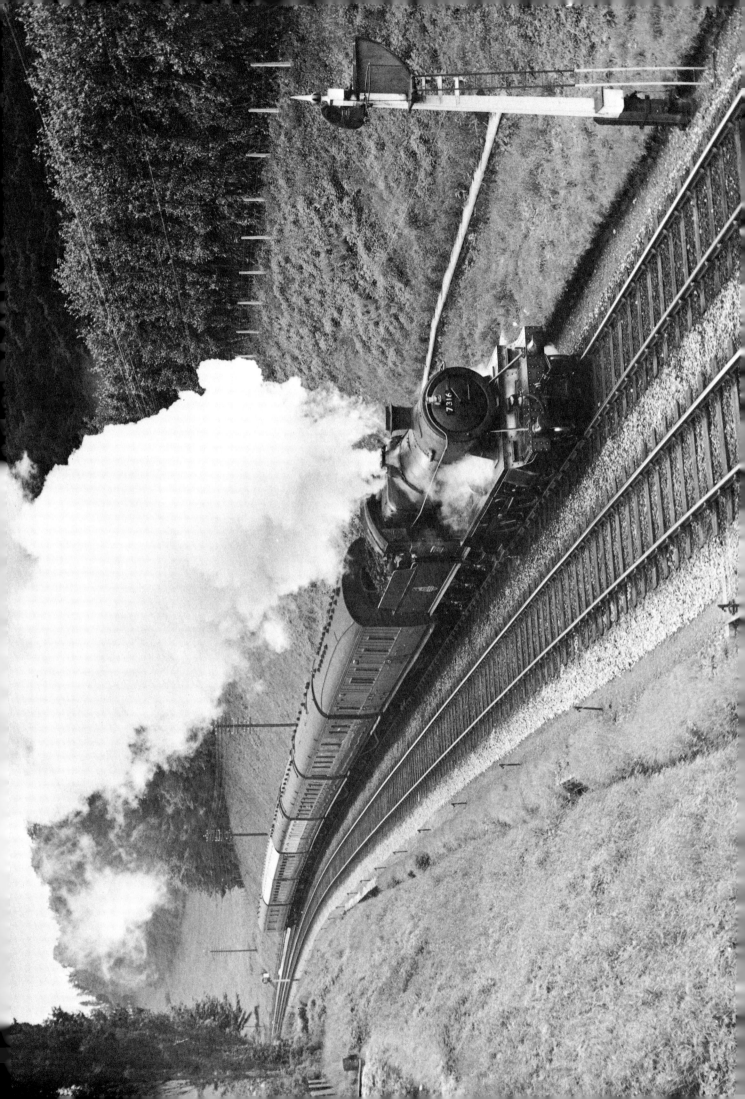

41 At Aller Junction a very mixed "up" train comes off the Plymouth line headed by No. 7809 **Childrey Manor** and an unidentified "Hall" class engine.
24 May 1958

42 I have included this one mainly because of the signals. It is a peaceful scene with No. 6028 **King George VI** held by the signals and the fireman up on the tender pushing coal forward. We saw this engine in picture thirty-eight on its way to London the day before. I wonder if it came back via Bristol, picking up Midland stock in the process.
24 May 1958

43 A final picture of my last Saturday in Devon, another peaceful scene taken from the Teignmouth-Newton Abbot road in the late evening and looking across the River Teign.
The Mogul is No. 6398 with automatic tablet exchange apparatus fitted to the tender which may

...organised a special train from Exeter to Penzance hauled by No. 3440 **City of Truro**. With standard B.R. stock it is climbing the 1 in 36 of Dainton Bank unaided.
25 May 1958

...of Dainton Tunnel with steam shut off and piloted by No. 7813 **Freshford Manor** which has a higher sided 3500 gallon tender. No. 7022 **Hereford Castle**, with double chimney, will most likely take the train on from Newton Abbot to Bristol.
25 May 1958

47 As it was a Sunday and there were not too many trains about, I drove over to Exeter to have a look round the shed and in particular to see the 16.10 Plymouth-Paddington. As you can see, the sun situation was uncertain to say the least, but it shone at the right moment as No. 6029 **King Edward VIII** came out of Exeter and approached Cowley Bridge Junction. Note the fine selection of signals and point rodding mounted on the concrete blocks.
25 May 1958

4[?] [...] to [...] of the [...]vation, movement running with single chimney and working a lightweight train up to Dainton and on to Plymouth No. 7029 **Clun Castle**, passes a distant signal with wooden arm. It continued its volcanic smoke effect until it disappeared from view the other side of Stonycombe Quarries.
25 May 1958

48 In the falling light of a late spring evening we see what I would say was a perfect Great Western scene. Exeter shed with the south end of St. Davids station visible in the background. The line up to Exeter Central is also visible and further comment is not necessary — just admire the state of the engines. **25 May 1958**

49 On the left is an ash wagon and two "Halls" stand in the middle awaiting work on the next day. A typical shed scene! **25 May 1958**

50 2-8-0 No. 2846 stands motionless at the stop blocks in front of the water tank and steam raising boilers. This engine was built in 1912 and was the first of the class to have heavy castings added to the framing to improve weight distribution and adhesion. It was also the last of the class to receive a smokebox number plate seven and a half years after nationalisation and was withdrawn two and a half

51 Exeter St. Davids station looking north with No. 1000 **County of Middlesex** leaving for Plymouth with a goodly set of Great Western stock. The old station stands out clearly and careful inspection will show a gas lamp at the middle platform and quite an array of backing signals.   **25 May 1958**

52 In picture number forty-five engine No. 7022 was seen with a Sunday excursion and here it is coming back in the evening passing Cowley Bridge Junction, where the Barnstaple road out of Exeter crosses on one of those brick skew bridges. These always fascinate me as I find it difficult enough to lay even a straight wall.   **25 May 1958**

53 I have included this picture as it is a well-known location to holidaymakers caught in the summer traffic jams — where the main line passes under the Exeter by-pass. The two large transept towers of Exeter's thirteenth century Cathedral are prominent on the sky-line.

No. 6027 **King Richard I** on the 15.30 Paddington-Plymouth express accelerates past a herd of cows, as the fireman is preparing to pick up water at the troughs beyond the village of Exminster.

54 Now my last day in Devon and this photograph is taken looking out to sea at Horse Cove, a location not often visited by photographers as it is difficult to find, there being no seawall access. A seagull glides over the sea above the elegant double chimney of No. 6008 **King James II** as it runs past with the up "Royal Duchy". **26 May 1958**

55 Looking round from picture **54** is a view so well known in Great Western publicity that I feel almost guilty in trespassing where many official photographers have trod. No. 5074 **Hampden** was visible after passing Dawlish Warren and Dawlish station can be seen in the background. Although the coaches are British Rail, they were painted in "Chocolate and Cream".

56 Usually "King"-hauled, the 09.10 Paddington-Birkenhead has No. 6979 **Helperly Hall** and No. 7024 **Powis Castle** in charge as they come out of the "Dip" between Leamington and Warwick. The Leamington parish church is visible above the bridge but perhaps this is the only railway photograph ever taken with a bird flying straight through the exhaust of the leading engine. It is not damaged emulsion on the negative as you

57 2-8-0 No. 48430 has a loaded iron-ore train for Brymbo steel works and is climbing unaided up the loop on Hatton Bank on its way from Banbury. Nineteen wagons was the limit for engines without a banker.

The driver of No. 4997 **Elton Hall** has seen me and both the crew are looking back along the train to see that all is well as they descend the 1 in 110

shire Union canal, which makes its way through the centre of Chester. It is interesting to compare the caravan and Standard Vanguard with the modern machinery seen on the roads today.
9 August 1958

upon them how stupid it was! Both the platelayers hut and tall distant signal for Leamington have been removed but, fortunately, No. 6000 **King George V** is still with us (but no longer working the 17.33 Wolverhampton-Paddington express).
16 August 1958

60 A load of Midland stock, probably a holiday extra, passes Fosse Box on its way south behind No. 5044 **Earl of Dunraven**. 2-8-0 No. 2847 has just emerged from Caerphilly works where it has been repainted, the safety valve bonnet has been polished and the reversing rod is now bright red. This engine, shedded at Cardiff Canton, was one of 20 to be converted to oil burning between October 1947 to June 1949.

61 One of my favourite "King" pictures with No. 6001 **King Edward VII** approaching Fosse Box with the 11.35 Wolverhampton-Paddington express visible just to the right of the engine on the skyline is the tall boiler house chimney at the Automotive Products Group factory at Leamington Spa.

deepest cuttings made at the time of its construction and this is a view taken from the brick bridge well known to enthusiasts, although I have never seen photographs taken from here. British Rail stock monopolised the trains at this time and No. 6013 **King Henry VIII** has a thirteen coach load in various liveries making up its Sunday Morning excursion.

31 August 1958

63 The next six pictures were taken during the Midland Area Stephenson Locomotive Society outing to Swindon. No. 7808 **Cookham Manor** stands outside Gloucester shed from where (at this period) it was working the M.S.W.J. line. It does not look as if they will be short of fuel on the next trip!

7 September 1958

leigh by No. 4900 **Saint Martin** and here it is shown in the Autumn sunshine standing in the sidings at Gloucester, while the passengers visited the shed. The tower of Gloucester Cathedral is clearly visible in the background.   **7 September 1958**

65 Auto fitted 0-4-2T No. 1424 awaits its next turn of duty beside a pannier tank with a very battered steam dome cover. The universal coupling for connection to the regulator rod below the Auto-Coach is clearly visible to the right and below the coupling hook. Note the two sand funnels used for filling locomotive sand boxes leaning against the shed.   **7 September 1958**

66 A general view outside the shed with two 2-8-0 "Austerity" engines on the right and a Great Western steam crane on the left.   **7 September 1958**

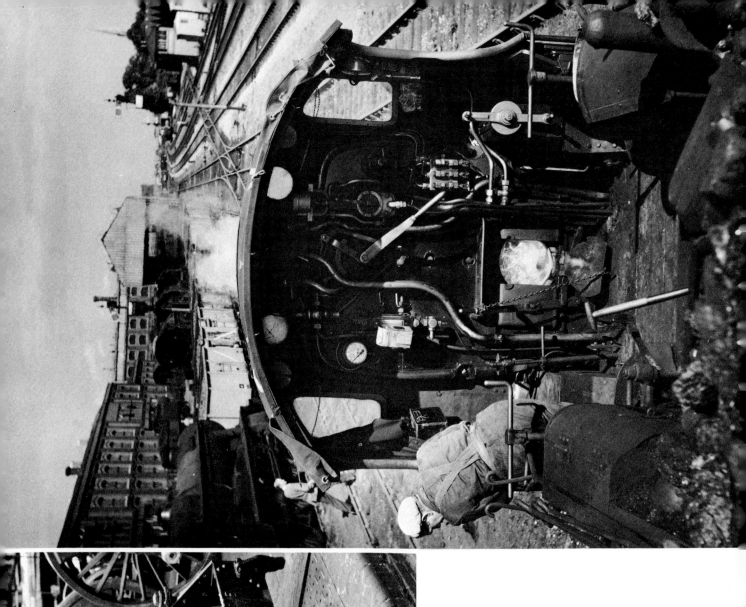

67 "Warships" under construction alongside steam engine manufacture and repair, but the bogie from No. 6024 **King Edward I** took my fancy on this occasion as it is of such a unique design. Clearly shown are the coil springs introduced after the Midgham derailment with No. 6003 and designed to soften the springing in conjunction with spring changes on the trailing coupled wheels.
7 September 1958

68 **City of Truro** as seen from the pile of coal in the tender and looking towards Swindon station from the sidings outside "A" shop. The chimney is barely visible through the steam coming from the safety valves. On the left is a "County" class engine with "Castles" in front awaiting repair.
7 September 1958

69 Although of Great Western origin, the Engineers Inspection Saloon was built by British Rail, and is coming through Leamington the day after the S.L.S. trip. I wonder if this was an excuse to use **City of Truro** for a run

70 I have a passion for Churchward's 2-8-0's and it is so seldom that a clean one came along that this picture is an obvious choice for this book. No. 3809, shedded at Cardiff Canton, has been priming, judging by the dribbles at the bottom of the smokebox. The location is Whitnash just south of Leamington and I think the engine is hauling an up coal train.

22 September 1959

71 One of the worst problems with steam railway photography was the exhaust drifting over the side of the engine if the wind was blowing towards the camera. This is such a case where there could have been trouble as the south-west wind is blowing into my face but luckily No. 6028 **King George VI** has just shut off steam and has the blower on. The train is the 09.10 Paddington-Birkenhead express, running down into Leamington.

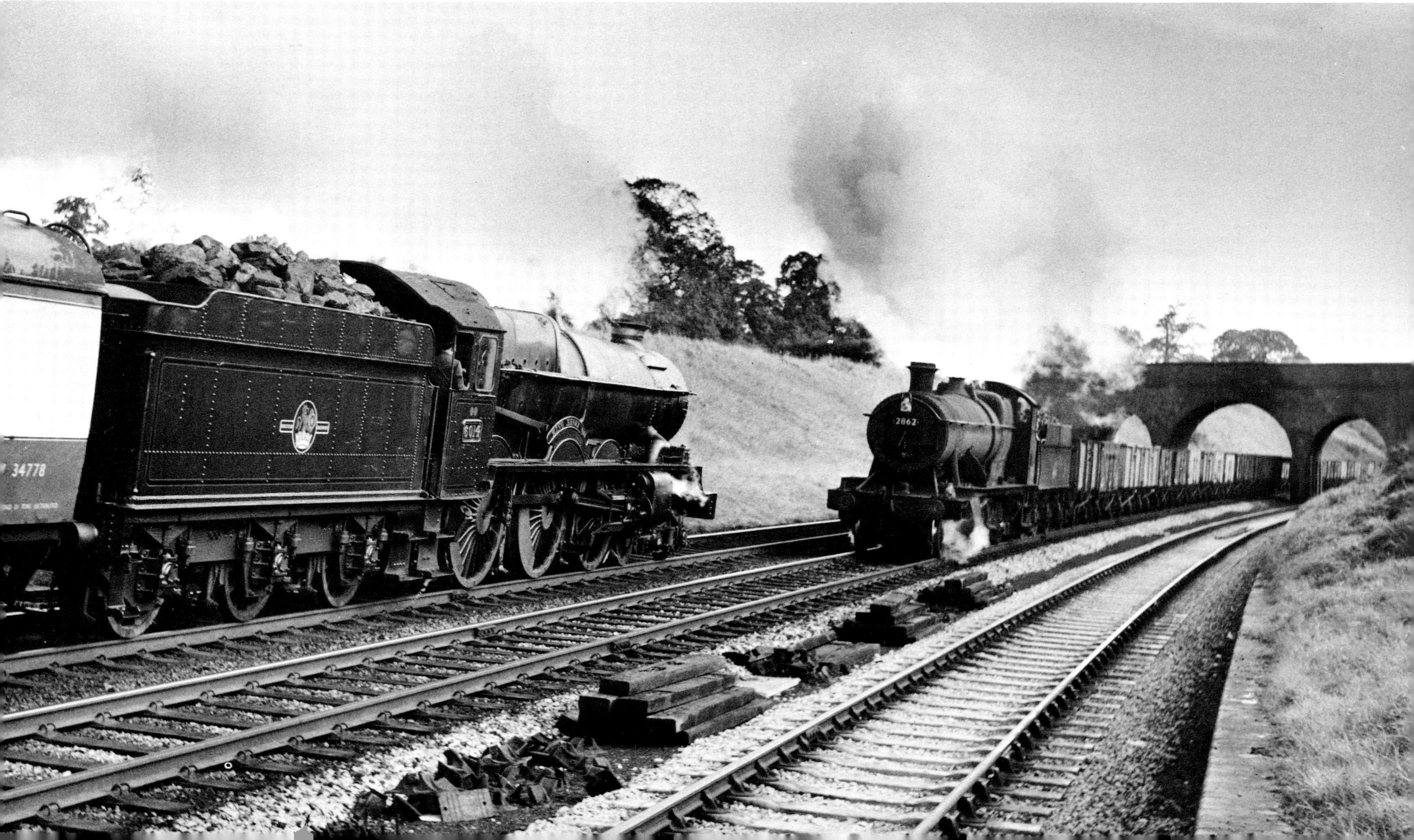

formance but purely for its appearance and sound. This engine was borrowed from Gloucester shed to work the Talyllyn Railway Special from Paddington to Shrewsbury seen here at the top of Hatton Bank.

No. [illegible] has a train of empty coal wagons and No. [illegible]4 King **Henry VII** flashes by on its way up to London with the 09.35 Wolverhampton to Paddington express. The roof of the coach has had a soaking during the water pick-up on Lapworth Troughs and you will also notice the enormous lumps of coal in the tender.

No. 2862 was also one of the twenty in the class converted to oil burning and ran in this state between 1946 and 1948. **6 October 1958**

... a second ... to ... provide a actual light source when detail in the shadows is required and in this picture the wheels are well illuminated. No. 6811 **Cranbourne Grange** and No. 5982 **Harrington Hall** have just passed Twyford with a train for Paddington. **11 October 1958**

09.00 remained the same, the timing to Snow Hill varied over the years, the shortest being two hours. In this picture No. 6003 **King George IV** is seen working very hard at the summit of Hatton Bank and with the final design of multi-coloured headboard. **6 October 1958**

76 No. 6147 was one of the 6100 class of 2-6-2T's built to work the accelerated London suburban services and were almost all allocated to sheds in that division. You will notice, just behind the centre driving wheel, the trip gear for automatic brake application in case of passing a signal at danger on the electrified lines. This would apply the brakes automatically. External sliding cab shutters are fitted. This broadside view was taken near Twyford.

11 October 1958

77 I have included this picture not because I particularly like it but as it was part of the scene, although it was touch and go at this date if it would be diesel or steam. There were only five of the AIA-AIA Warship class built by North British Locomotive Co. and this one, No. 600 **Active**, has at least three men riding in the cab.

11 October 1958

78 Surely the most handsome of the standard British Rail engines and particularly so with the double chimney. Judging by the 86A shed plate on the smokebox door, the train headed by 2-10-0 No. 92239 will be on its way down to South Wales. Notice that the signals are off for the up and down main and, of course, the down relief as well.

11 October 1958

...towards the end of October the sun is so low in the sky at midday, that in the middle of Hatton cutting the down main line is in shadow; but the up, although descending here, is still good for photography as shown by a Permanent Way train being hauled away from Hatton station by 0-6-0 No. 2230.
25 October 1958

month, No. 4900 **Saint Martin** has an up empty of iron ore wagons, probably for Banbury. I saw the train in Leamington station for the first picture and then drove up to Southam Road and Harbury station where as you can see, the fireman was busy at work.
18 October 1958

81 Looking south on Hatton Bank we have on the left a motor car train made up mainly of "Mogo" 4-wheel wagons with end loading and probably going to Morris Cowley, Oxford. On the down loop No. 6971 **Athelhampton Hall** toils up the gradient with a down freight.
10 January 1959

82 Half an hour later the 11.35 Wolverhampton-Paddington express with steam shut off sweeps by on a snowy afternoon. Compare this picture with a similar one taken on 19th of January 1955 in my first book *Shadows of the Great Western.*
10 January 1959

83 It may not look too cold as there is only a sprinkling of snow on the ground in Warwick Goods yard, but you can tell from the smoke that there is an east wind blowing which also means plenty of steam coming my way from the inside cylinders. The arch of the bridge makes a nice frame for No. 6006 **King George I** as it starts the climb away from Warwick station with the 11.10 from Paddington.
10 January 1959

Royal Star, heads for London while No. 5043, **Earl of Mount Edgcumbe,** is Swindon bound. The location is a mile west of Twyford where the line is on an embankment, and the ballast box makes a suitable table for my two wooden camera boxes. 35 mm. is much easier. **28 February 1959**

85 Just on the London side of Old Oak Common No. 5057 **Earl Waldegrave** nears the end of its journey on the up main, rapidly overtaking No. 6929 **Whorlton Hall** on the up relief line. **21 March 1959**

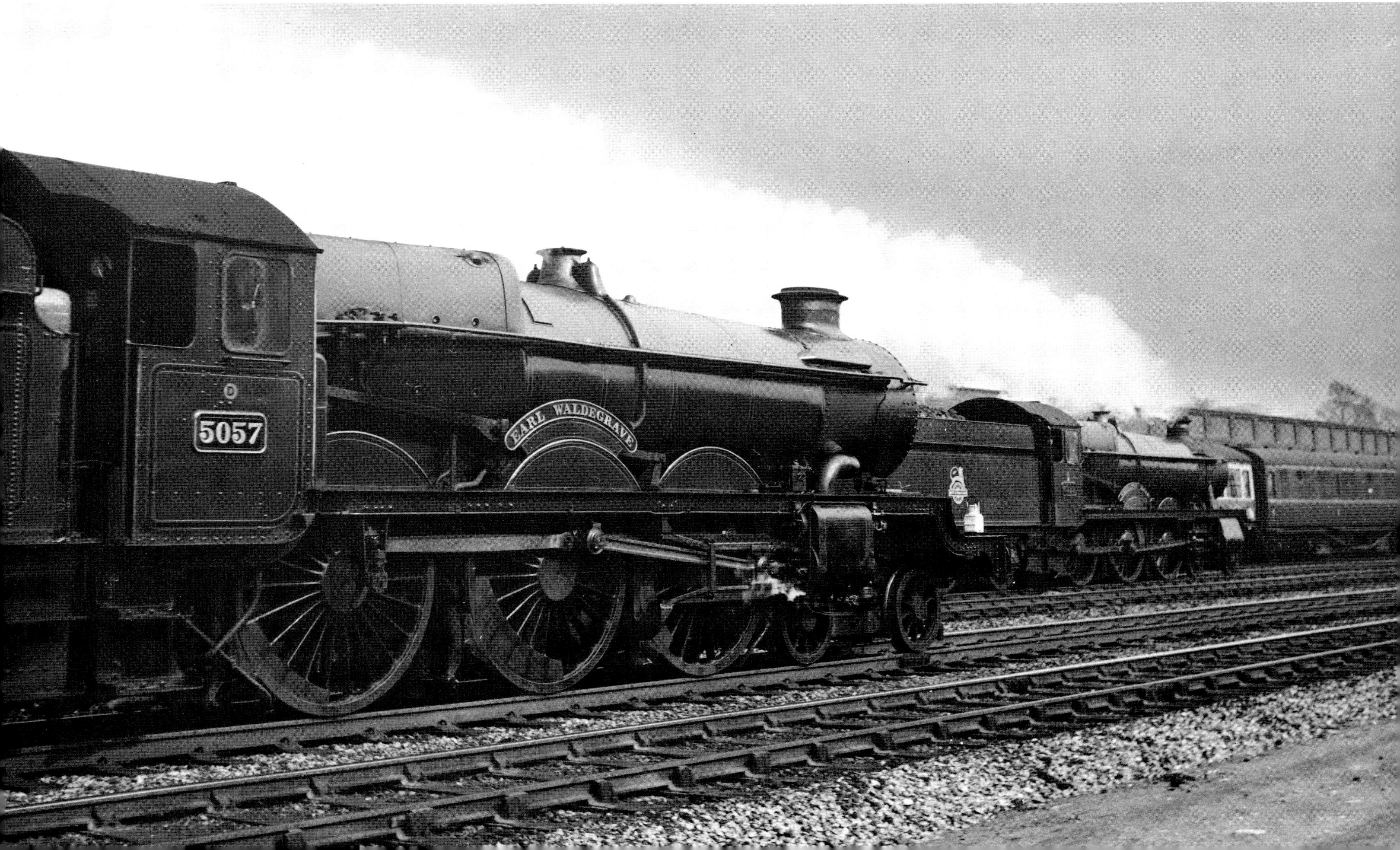

86 "Britannia" Pacific No. 70022 **Tornado** takes shelter under Bishop's Bridge Road at the end of Platform 3 at Paddington station. It is awaiting the green flag for its journey to Cardiff.
21 March 1959

87 The chances of a steam-hauled "Cornish Riviera" were small at this time; probably the diesel had failed before leaving Laira shed and a "King" was quickly substituted, together with the old style of headboard. No. 6007 **King William III** stands at the buffer stops of Paddington's No. 8 platform. Here is no diesel pollution or continually noisy running engine — just the sweet smell of a hot and oily steam engine with the blower gently "cracked on".
21 March 1959

88 Platforms 1 and 2 at Paddington occupied by No. 6136 on a semi-fast to Reading, while No. 6025 **King Henry III** waits patiently for the "right

89 The "Mayflower" has now departed and we get a better picture of No. 6136 with its elegant copper-capped chimney. Dusk is falling rapidly as the camera now demands a tripod.
21 March 1959

90 Looking out of the station along Platform 2 we have No. 6017 **King Edward IV** waiting to leave with the 18.10 Paddington-Wolverhampton express for the North.
21 March 1959

No. 7005 **Sir Edward Elgar** was named after the composer during his Centenary Year in 1957. The train is seen here leaving Worcester. The road bridge in the background carries the main road from Worcester to Evesham. The state of the engine is so typical of the day to day turn-out produced by Worcester shed.

9 April 1959

92 In Sonning Cutting the down "Royal Duchy" 13.30 from Paddington is headed by "Warship" class No. D.800 **Sir Brian Robertson**, but the object of interest is 0-6-0PT No. 5746, which I am afraid was a definite loser in the race to Reading!

31 March 1959

93 Here we have a combination of engines and stock as I have never seen before or since. The train is the 11.35 Wolverhampton-Paddington express with a complete rake of Southern stock hauled by No. 5019 **Treago Castle** and No. 6020 **King Henry IV**. I cannot find a reason for the coaches but probably the "Castle" was working "up to town" to help bring back an extra train for the Easter holiday. Location—Harbury Cutting.

26 March 1959

94 I spent a number of years travelling overseas and this entailed staying a night in London before flying off early the next day. It did however have an advantage in that I could wander around Paddington at night, and here we see a "castle" from Landore shed standing at Platform 8. My records for once have failed to provide the engine name.

30 April 1959

95 2-6-2T No. 6151 stands at the buffers sheltering from the night and allowing the crew to have a well earned cup of tea. **30 April 1959**

96 We now come to a scene at Paddington which was to disappear over the years when the diesels would remove steam altogether from Brunel's masterpiece. No. D.802 **Formidable** stands in Platform 10 and No. 6027 **King Richard I** is about to back out of the station after its train has been moved out by an engine at the other end. **1 May 1959**

97 Crossing the Princes Drive bridge in Leamington is the 17.10 Paddington-Wolverhampton express double-headed by a class 4 No. 75026 and No. 6014 **King Henry VII**.

98 Quite a dramatic smoke effect but not requested by me on this occasion! No. 5046 **Earl Cawdor** pulls out of Stratford-on-Avon with the "Cornishman" from Penzance to Wolverhampton. A Collett 0-6-0 gives a helping hand for the climb up to Wilmcote. The pilot came on at Leamington to assist during the climb at 1 in 45 **26 May 1959**

hot summer day when shadows are black, without any reflected light from a cloudless sky. Knowle and Dorridge station is the location as No. 6010 **King Charles I** flashes through on the ''Up Cambrian'' and past a nice example of Great Western signal manufacture. **17 June 1959**

100 No. 4085 **Berkeley Castle** and No. 5094 **Tretower Castle** double-head the up Cheltenham Spa express through Sonning Cutting. Notice the nicely built platelayers hut with various tools leaning on the outside wall.

These two engines worked back together on a down express during the afternoon. **25 July 1959**

101 Hardly of Great Western origin, but seen by thousands of passengers as it shunted coal wagons in and out of Earley Power Station, situated on the up side of the main line just before Sonning Cutting. The engine is works No. 7058 of 1942 built by Robert Stephenson and Hawthorne, Newcastle upon Tyne, and at the time of writing is standby to a diesel locomotive. **25 July 1959**

102 Another "panned" picture in the depths of Sonning Cutting after the sun had disappeared behind a thin veil of cloud.
    The engine is No. 70018 **Flying Dutchman** with the down **"Red Dragon"**.   **25th July 1959**

103 No. 7000 **Viscount Portal** passes the well-known set of signals at Scours Lane, Reading, with the down Cheltenham Spa express.   **25 July 1959**

104 We are looking across the estuary of the Mawddach with the sea front of Barmouth just visible on the left through the haze. Just above the top of the tender of the Collett 0-6-0 can be seen 4-4-2 **Count Louis** on the Fairbourne Miniature Railway and above the fourth carriage of the up Cambrian Coast express is another train crossing Barmouth viaduct in the distance. A Gresley coach in maroon livery is sandwiched between the British Rail stock which is in chocolate and cream livery. **2 September 1959**

105 A Collett 0-6-0 is just visible in the carriage sidings on the left as two 4-6-0 class 4's, No. 75026 and No. 75005 leave Machynlleth with the up "Cambrian Coast Express". **1 September 1959**

106 The Dukedog is blowing off furiously as the fireman pulls down some coal in the tender and two fitters are at work underneath the front end of No. 7011 **Banbury Castle.**

The vacuum brake pipe and inside cylinder outer cover have been removed, but more than anything else I like the outfit of tools, various hammers and crowbars, lying on either side of the track.

The location is Shrewsbury shed as I am sure you have guessed. **26 September 1959**

107 This view shows the two Dukedogs, No. 9004 and No. 9014, being prepared on Shrewsbury shed for the Talyllyn Railway Special train which they would take on from Shrewsbury to Towyn. The Abbey Church of the Holy Cross could have provided a wonderful platform for steam railway photography.
26 September 1959

108 "X" number boards signify a special and here it is held by the signals at the entrance to the triangle with the Abbey Foregate Curve, complete with check rails going off to the right. No. 7007 **Great Western** has an eight-coach train with members of the Talyllyn Railway Preservation Society. To the left can be seen the tender of No. 5032 **Usk Castle** waiting to take a train to London, and there is also a 2-6-2T under the signal gantry on the right of the picture.
26 September 1959

climb into the Welsh mountains with the I.R.P.S. special.

26 September 1959

dred and five taken earlier in the month, but in this case the headboard has been put on the first engine. Both are pulling hard on the climb up to Talerddig with a combined tractive effort of 50,200 lbs.

26 September 1959

26 September 1959

111 Later in the afternoon the down Cambrian Coast Express has arrived at Machynlleth, and the front part continued on to Aberystwyth behind an immaculate No. 7802 **Bradley Manor.** The rear portion will travel round the coast to Pwllheli behind this 2-6-2T No. 5540, which was withdrawn for scrapping within a year of this picture being taken. Have a good look at the architecture and the bridge in the foreground, under which is the A487.
26 September 1959

112 It was about this time that preservation of a Dukedog got underway and this is the engine which now runs on the Bluebell Railway. No. 9017 is moving backwards and forwards in the sidings for photographs to be taken. The end of a P.W. mess van is visible on the right.
26 September 1959

113 After the T.R.P.S. special arrived at Towyn the Dukedogs made their way back to Machynlleth shed, No. 9014 running light and No. 9004 seen here piloting a class 2 2-6-0 on a mixed freight. They are ambling along the coastline of the Dovey estuary in the late evening sunlight.
26 September 1959

114 A late afternoon study of Machynlleth shed with, from left to right No. 78005, No. 5565 and No. 5510. The site for the shed had to be blasted out of solid rock. To the left of the signal box the tracks led down to the exchange sidings with the former Corris Narrow Gauge Railway.
26 September 1959

115 If you look out of the window after passing Warwick opposite the Warwick Race Course stands the cold storage plant. Although now denuded of its rail connection I was lucky enough to see No. 5927 **Guild Hall** shunting in the yard on a fine October morning having left its pick-up freight in the freight loop.
14 October 1959

116 No. 75023 is running into Worcester Shrub Hill station with a stopping train from Birmingham, and a "Hall" is backing out of the down platform to go on to shed.
11 November 1959

117

When looking through the pictures in this book you may be led to believe that the steam locomotive never broke down. Well it did and these four pictures show what happened when the driver of the 09.10 Paddington-Birkenhead decided that he had had enough of his engine No. 6027 **King Richard I.**

119

118

In photograph 117 we see the "King" coming off the train in the down platform at Leamington Spa. In photo 118 the "King" is in a siding on the right and the station pilot No. 4118 with express headlamps, leaves for Birmingham unassisted.

The "King" then retired to Leamington shed, where in photo 119 it is being looked at by the shed staff. In 120 it moves up and down the yard after what appeared to be a satisfactory repair. **28 November 1959**

120

121 As a farewell to main line steam in 1959 we can see No. 6012 **King Edward VI** coming through the centre road at Leamington station with the down Cambrian Coast Express. **5 December 1959**

122 The L.N.W.R. signal box controlling the junction with the G.W.R. is shown behind 0-6-0PT No. 2067 standing in a siding outside Leamington shed. Although you may not be able to see it, someone has written in chalk on the chimney "2000°F" and "Nimrod" on the smokebox.

This engine was built in 1899 and converted to pannier tanks in 1919, and was withdrawn in 1952. Incredibly it survived for steam-raising purposes **at** the back of Leamington shed until 1959 when pre-sumably it went for scrapping. I wonder if this engine was the last of the "2021" class to be cut up?
5 December 1959

Silhouettes of the GREAT WESTERN

R. J. BLENKINSOP

Published by:
Oxford Publishing Co.
Link House
West Street
POOLE, Dorset

Printed in Great Britain by:
Netherwood Dalton & Co. Ltd., Huddersfield, Yorks.

1   I am starting the book with one of the fastest trains on the Western Region. The 13.15 Paddington-Bristol was allowed two hours for the 118¼ miles, including a stop at Bath. No. 6015 **King Richard III** was travelling over 70 m.p.h. when this photograph was taken at the west end of Sonning Cutting, near Reading.

19 April 1960

2 Both engines seem to be taking water at the same time quite satisfactorily in this scene at Goring troughs. With a load of 14 bogies No. 5051 **Earl Bathurst** has No. 5980 **Dingley Hall** as pilot with an afternoon express from Paddington to Bristol.

19 April 1960

3 In making my way westwards towards Didcot a country road crosses the main line adjacent to Moreton yard some 1½ miles east of Didcot station.

In the low evening sun No. 7035 **Ogmore Castle** is in charge of the "Cheltenham Spa Express" which had its first stop at Kemble. The double chimney on the "Castles" never looked right although I must have photographed it from every conceivable angle.

19 April 1960

4

2-8-0 No. 4705 is seen leaving Didcot for Swindon with a stopping train, having departed from Reading at 17.16. The engine looks fairly clean so was probably on a return "running in" turn from Swindon.

The bedraggled engine on the left of the picture is No. 4078 **Pembroke Castle** waiting at the signals with an up freight.

19 April 1960

5

While the express passenger train had all the glory shed on it – usually because it was fast and clean – I often preferred the fascination of the goods train rattling past with its variety of wagons and load.

In this scene No. 4946 **Moseley Hall** passes Croes Newydd shed with an up freight carrying class "K" headlamps.

30 April 1960

"Dukedog" No. 9014 in the yard outside Croes Newydd shed.
Allocated to Oswestry shed No. 7827 **Lydham Manor** has just taken on water
for the first leg of the journey to Pwllheli.

30 April 1960

7

In this picture the pair are moving off shed on their way to Ruabon to take over
a special train of members of the Festiniog Railway Preservation Society.

30 April 1960

8　No. 1021 **County of Montgomery** crosses a new set of points with flat bottom
track at Llangollen line junction just to the south of Ruabon. It will have worked
all the way from London, to return in the early hours of Sunday morning with
two sleeping cars added to the formation. This photograph clearly shows the
highest part of a Great Western engine.

30 April 1960

9   After the engine change at Ruabon the "Manor" and "Dukedog" are seen at the west end of Corwen goods yard with the road bridge in the background carrying the A5 on its way to Holyhead.

30 April 1960

10 I believe Inspector Jack Hancock is silhouetted standing on the far side of the footplate just after the train has passed Llanuwchllyn station. Arrival at Minffordd was some 15 minutes before the advertised time.

30 April 1960

11 On our overcrowded roads today chasing trains is hazardous but with little traffic about in April of that year my Morris Minor was clearly the faster of the two means of transport. I am sure the bird is a seagull but why black I do not know. Anyway it adds to the nautical atmosphere as the train comes off the bridge and into Barmouth.

30 April 1960

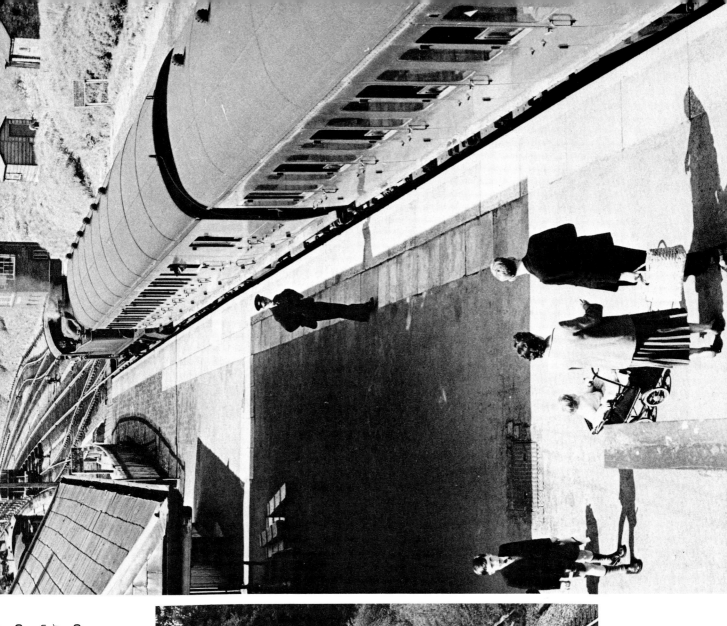

Welsh mountains.

30 April 1960

13 Taken from the passenger footbridge at Southam Road and Harbury Station an afternoon local train from Banbury to Leamington is just leaving, with the porter about to take the tickets from the passengers in the foreground.

6 May 1960

14 Southam Road and Harbury Station was over a mile from Harbury village and even farther to Southam. In this view taken in 1974 a "Western" class diesel Hydraulic passes the site of the former station and goods yard.

It is interesting to compare the two pictures on this page as only the hut for the P.W. gang remains and at the time of writing this class of diesel will not be with us much longer.

16 July 1974

6 May 1960

ascending the gradient with the up "Cambrian Coast Express".

14 May 1960

16 With the arrival of the diesel a number of "King" class engines were allocated to Cardiff Canton shed to work the South Wales expresses to London. No. 6009 **King Charles II** passes Little Somerford station at high speed with the driver and fireman looking out of the cab. The 702 reporting numbers covered the 08.30 Cardiff to Paddington.

17 A delightful scene not expected on the main line, but standing in the down platform at Little Somerford on a glorious spring morning is a pick-up freight from Swindon with 0-4-2T No. 5815 in charge. The goods yard layout is of interest and also the double slip points on the down line above the guard's van.

14 May 1960

The sun shone through the stormy sky as the train came up the 1 in 400 gradient at 83 m.p.h. and running nearly 15 minutes ahead of time. In fact, the train was so early that a number of enthusiasts missed it, having come many miles armed with cameras to see "his majesty" hard at work.

14 May 1960

20　The "Severn and Wessex Express" ran from Paddington to Severn Tunnel Junction and back to Bath for a journey over the Somerset and Dorset line.
　　Here, 2-6-0 No. 6384 runs into Bath past the shed where S. and D. 2-8-0 No. 53807 awaits to take the train to Bournemouth.

14 May 1960

19　No. 6912 **Helmster Hall** is working hard on the climb up to Wootton Bassett with an up fast freight train comprising mainly of coal from South Wales. There is plenty of detail visible in the signals for the railway modellers.

14 May 1960

21 On the way home from Bath I again halted at Wootton Bassett and saw two trains take the South Wales main line. No. 4094 **Dynevor Castle** has just come off the main line from Paddington to Bath and the signalman has certainly returned the signals to danger very quickly. Notice the old guard's van on the right of the picture leading a retired life away from all the activity.

14 May 1960

22 The signals are those as shown in picture No. 19 and it looks as if No. 6820 **Kingstone Grange** is fresh from overhaul at Swindon works before returning to its home shed at Worcester.

14 May 1960

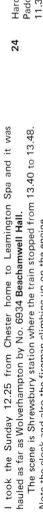

23 I took the Sunday 12.25 from Chester home to Leamington Spa and it was hauled as far as Wolverhampton by No. 6934 **Beachamwell Hall.**
The scene is Shrewsbury station where the train stopped from 13.40 to 13.48. Note the clock and also the fireman climbing up on the engine.

26 June 1960

24 Hardly necessary for a caption to this photograph so it must be platform 10 at Paddington station and shows No. 6006 **King George I** after arrival with the 11.35 from Wolverhampton.
The crew will be leaning out of the other side of the locomotive talking to any passengers who can't resist the temptation to stop and admire the machinery at

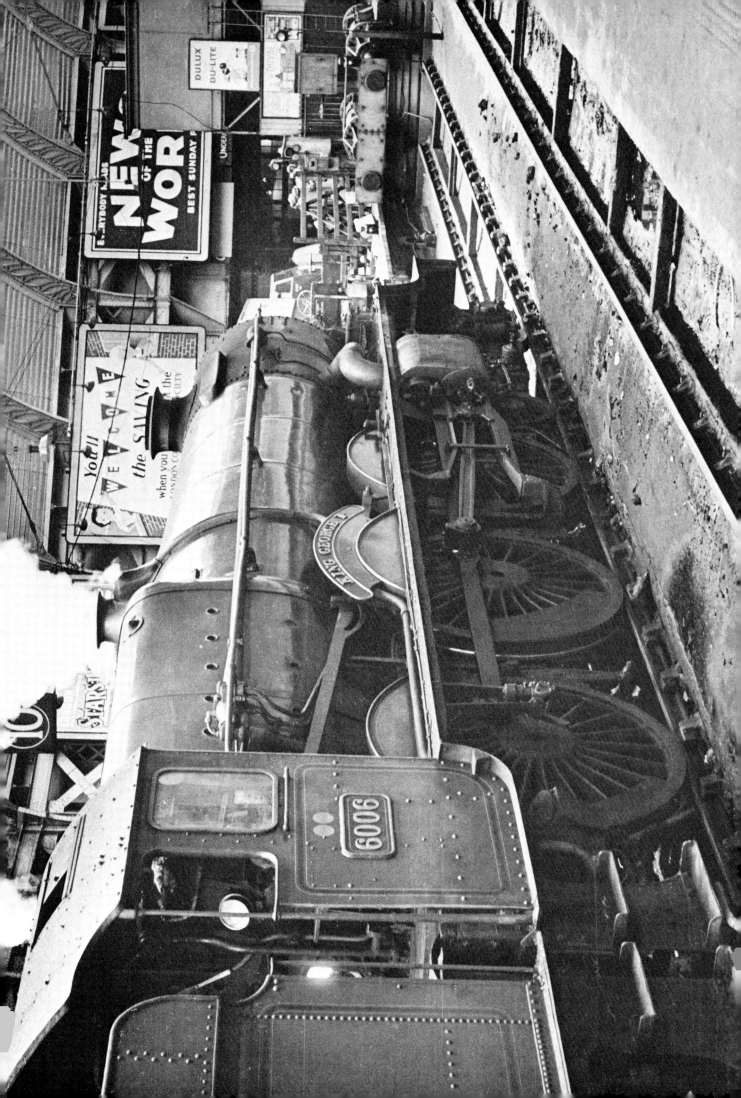

25   At this period between 08.30 and 20.10 there were no less than 14 express departures each weekday from Paddington to Wolverhampton via Bicester. Twelve of these had restaurant cars, and buffet cars were included in the other two. Today there is one train a day via Bicester.

No. 6015 **King Richard III** stands in Platform 2 with the 15.10 to Wolverhampton and was allowed 100 minutes for the non-stop run to Leamington Spa which is 87¼ miles from Paddington.

30 June 1960

26   I took this photograph as it is unusual to be able to study the top of the boiler of a "King" at rest. Notice the safety valves, cladding fittings, whistles, and ventilators in the cab roof together with the longitudinal taper of the firebox.

30 June 1960

27   A Sunday visit to Old Oak Common produced an interesting set of photographs including this one of No. 6012 **King Edward VI** standing by the coaling plant. It had worked the "Cambrian Coast Express" to Shrewsbury and back the day before. The pile of ashes and soot emphasize

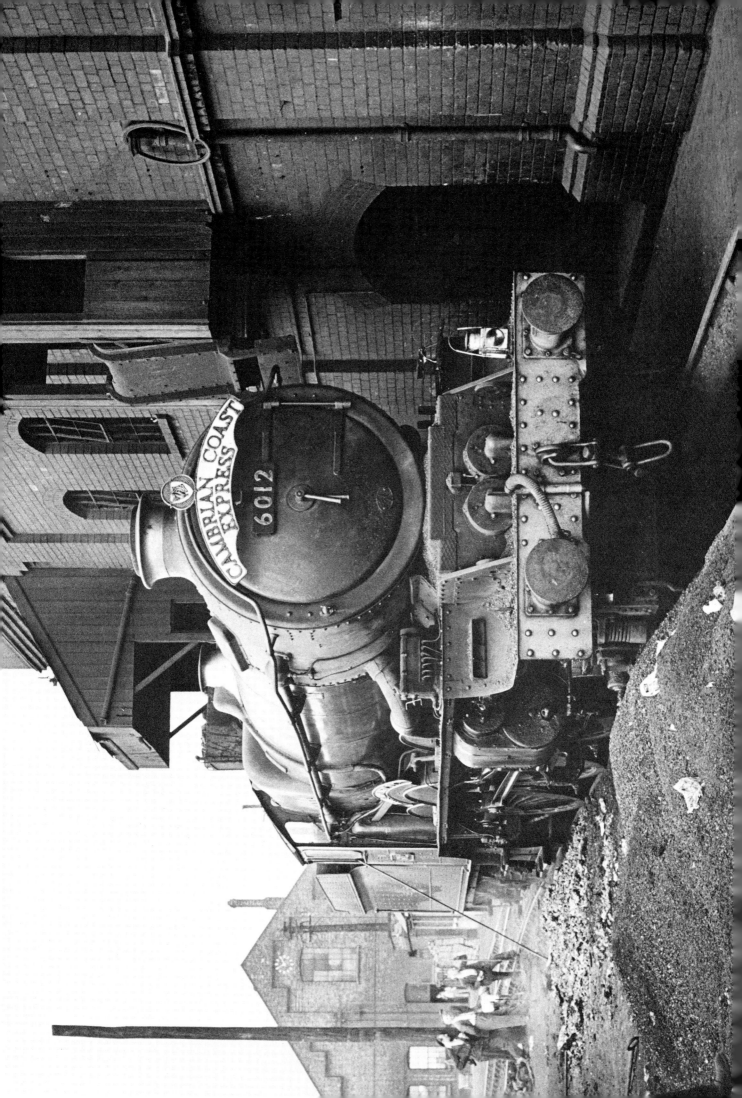

28   Out in the yard No. 6018 **King Henry VI** and No. 7017 **G.J. Churchward** await the next call of duty. The tender of the "Castle" is being replenished and if I remember correctly the "King" was on stand-by in case of any diesel failure.

3 July 1960

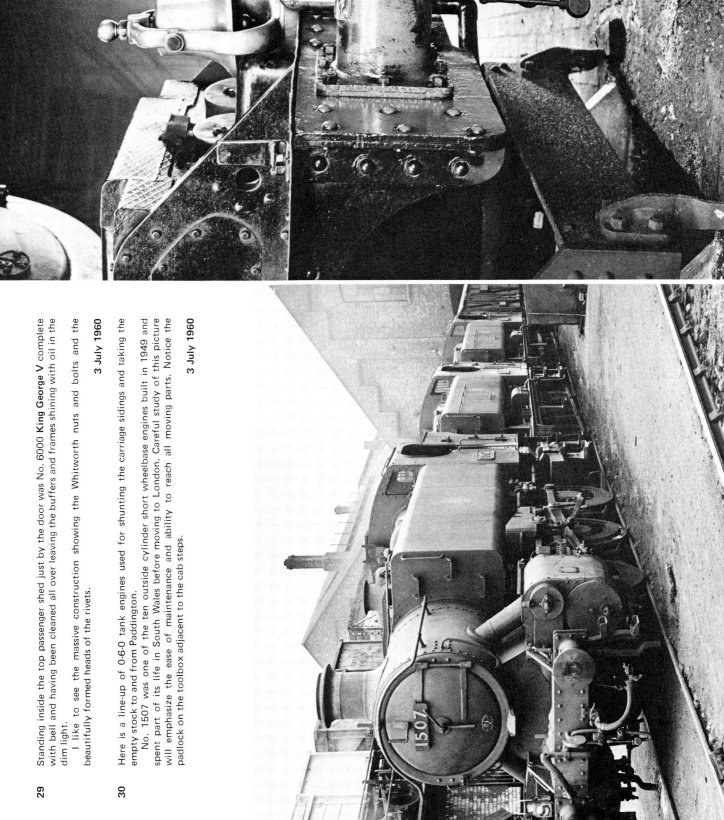

29 Standing inside the top passenger shed just by the door was No. 6000 **King George V** complete with bell and having been cleaned all over leaving the buffers and frames shining with oil in the dim light.

I like to see the massive construction showing the Whitworth nuts and bolts and the beautifully formed heads of the rivets.

3 July 1960

30 Here is a line-up of 0-6-0 tank engines used for shunting the carriage sidings and taking the empty stock to and from Paddington.

No. 1507 was one of the ten outside cylinder short wheelbase engines built in 1949 and spent part of its life in South Wales before moving to London. Careful study of this picture will emphasize the ease of maintenance and ability to reach all moving parts. Notice the padlock on the toolbox adjacent to the cab steps.

3 July 1960

31 At Old Oak Common the engines were cleaned inside the shed, and with its large allocation of express engines arranged around the four turntables, the atmosphere of living with steam engines was exhilarating.

This, the largest depot of the Great Western Railway, was built in 1906 and the view shows No. 6973 **Bricklehampton**

32

Superheater elements are leaning against the buffer beam of a member of the "4700" class followed by L.M.S. 2-8-0 No. 48431, No. 7903 **Foremarke Hall** and No. 6023 **King Edward II**.

The engines are stabled off the north turntable and looking due east, so readers can easily identify the location.

3 July 1960

33

Headboards galore are leaning against the shed office from where they are collected by the crew for fitting on the smoke-box lamp iron before leaving the depot. On the left are two samples of "The Merchant Venturer" 11.05 Paddington to Weston-super-Mare followed by the "Torbay Express" 12.00 Paddington-Kingswear and against the wall is the "South Wales Pullman" 08.50 Paddington to Swansea. The right side is not so easy with their riveted repairs. The "Inter-City" 09.00 Paddington to Wolverhampton followed by an unidentifiable headboard, probably "The Cambrian Coast Express". Leaning against the wall is the multi-coloured version of the "Inter-City".

3 July 1960

34   The final picture at Old Oak Common shows the south turntable and of particular interest is the 65 ft. under girder turntable which is completely boarded over to allow the staff easy access. The design of the roof is also of interest, bearing in mind that the size of the building is 360 ft. x 444 ft. From left to right can be seen No. 5981 **Frensham Hall**, No. 6973 **Brickle-**

35   No. 6000 **King George V**, seen here working the down "Cambrian Coast Express", on one of the fastest stretches of track covered during its journey. Fosse Box signal box is behind the engine and with the speed into the 80s the exposure was 1/1000 of a second at f4.

36

I hope this picture will give encouragement to those involved in restoring this fine engine at Quainton Road near Aylesbury. It is certainly in good condition here as it takes the up "Inter-City" on the embankment from Whitnash to Harbury.

15 July 1960

37

The Autumn special train to Swindon of the "Stephenson Locomotive Society" leaves Leamington Spa wrong line working on a Sunday morning. This was the last time I saw No. 3440 **City of Truro** in steam before it was withdrawn in May the following year for preservation in the Swindon Railway Museum.

4 September 1960

38

A view of Warwick goods yard looking north with 2-6-2T No. 5101 assisting an iron ore train at the beginning of Hatton Bank. The yard is now an oil storage complex, with all rail facilities and signals removed and a fence erected beside the down line.

As usual the train engine is one of the stalwarts of the G.W.R., namely a 2-8-0 No. 2874.

10 September 1960

and ex-works No. 5095 **Barbury Castle**.

11 September 1960

40   You may remember the long walk at Swindon Works along the side of the main line down to "A" shop. The first sight of an ex-works engine took place by a turntable out in the open. With a collection of ashpans on the right 2-8-0 No. 4701 and "Britannia" Pacific No. 70022 **Tornado** have been undergoing steam tests.

11 September 1960

Built in 1910 for use in dock areas where there are sharp curves 0-6-0 saddle tank No. 1365 ended its days at Swindon and is shown here next to the west turntable. Even though it appears to be "marked up" at a very low price this did not prevent it from being cut up after withdrawal in November 1962.

11 September 1960

42 Now beautifully preserved at Swindon Railway Museum, "Dean Goods" 0-6-0 No. 2516 awaits restoration as it stands outside Swindon works. Built in 1897 it survived two world wars and was withdrawn from Oswestry shed in May 1956.

11 September 1960

43 A contrast of beauty and functional design is apparent in this view outside "A" shop at Swindon works.

Originally built at Crewe 2-10-0 No. 92006 has just emerged from a major overhaul and together with No. 6019 **King Henry V** they are awaiting to be united with their tenders before steam tests and running in.

11 September 1960

44 This detail is a view of the rocking levers used to drive the outside piston valves on No. 6019 **King Henry V.**

Accessibility to the motion on four-cylinder Great Western engines was always a problem and this picture gives an idea of what it was all about.

11 September 1960

45 No. 4086 **Builth Castle** is under repair at Swindon works flanked by a "Mogul" and "Hall" class locomotive.

11 September 1960

Apart from No. 6008 **King James II** nearing the end of a major overhaul there is the frame and cab side of No. 7026 **Tenby Castle** and also one of the early "Warship" diesels. In the right foreground are stacked vacuum brake cylinders with piston rod protruding at the top.

11 September 1960

47 A study in chimney shapes outside Swindon shed with No. 4969 **Shrugborough Hall**, No. 1010 **County of Caernarvon**, Class B1 No. 61137 and 7022 **Hereford Castle**.

11 September 1960

48 No. 7811 **Dunley Manor** heads out of Shrewsbury and past the shed with a train for Aberystwyth. This lovely autumn day started with a thick mist and it was just beginning to clear when the picture was taken.

24 September 1960

49 As the mist lifts 2-6-0 No. 7330 moves out of Shrewsbury shed to take on water before working the "Talyllyn Railway Preservation Society Special" to Towyn.

24 September 1960

50 Just about to couple on to the "Mogul" is "Dukedog" No. 9017 now preserved on the Bluebell line. This engine, the last of the "Dukedogs" to run, was withdrawn the following month. They will always be remembered for the coupling rods which used to flash up and down in the sunlight when travelling at speed.

24 September 1960

51 Hauling the "Talyllyn Railway Preservation Society Special" from Paddington to Shrewsbury this 2-8-0 No. 4701 resplendent in lined-out green livery. It is shown here with steam shut off and coasting down into Shrewsbury.

Note the snifting valves on the outside of the steam chest which was standard on only four members of the class.

24 September 1960

52 As a farewell to the "Dukedogs" I must include this my last photograph of them, climbing away from Shrewsbury in the brilliant sunshine with a rake of B.R. stock.

24 September 1960

53 Soon after the "Talyllyn Railway Preservation Society Special" had departed I waited for the up "Cambrian Coast Express" which appeared behind No. 7818 **Granville Manor** and 0-6-0 No. 2200. The train continued to London behind No. 5059 **Earl St. Aldwyn** and after a mad dash to Upton Magna in the car I caught the train coming through in fine style on its way to Wolverhampton.

54 The down "Cambrian Coast Express" arrived in Shrewsbury behind No. **6015 King Richard III** and after an engine change it is seen here on its way to Aberystwyth behind No. **7818 Granville Manor.**

On a Saturday the rake of B.R. stock always had an ex-L.N.E.R. coach leading and I have never yet had an explanation for this unusual working.

24 September 1960

The breakdown crane is just visible on the right of the picture as 0-6-0PT No. 8781 shunts across the South Wales main line outside Shrewsbury shed.

24 September 1960

55

In the distance a passenger train disappears towards Chester and a "Hall" class engine is just visible under the road bridge. Meanwhile, on the right No. 1025 **County of Radnor** crosses the line leading out of Shrewsbury station for Crewe and the north-west.

An interesting example of trackwork is the reason for including this picture.

24 September 1960

56

Richard III which would shortly be returning to London with an afternoon express. After servicing and coaled up ready for the road the engine is seen leaving for Shrewsbury station.

24 September 1960

58 No. 7025 **Sudeley Castle** is having the ash removed from its smokebox after working the 08.00 Plymouth-Liverpool train. This engine, of course, comes off at Shrewsbury to be replaced by a London Midland engine for the journey onto Liverpool.

24 September 1960

59 A general view of Shrewsbury shed showing the Great Western Railway section on the left and the London Midland on the right. No. 4701 is awaiting to take the "Talyllyn Railway Preservation Society Special" back to London in the early hours of the next morning and No. 7821 **Ditcheat Manor** on a train from the Welsh coast is held at the signals, while a Class 5 can be seen taking on water.

24 September 1960

Manor, is an exception as it leaves Shrewsbury for Aberystwyth at 15.57 according to the clock on the Abbey. Note the complement of G.W.R. coaches.

24 September 1960

62 Newbury Races was always a great day for steam specials and the first on this Saturday morning was hauled by No. 7037 **Swindon.** Up above, as luck would have it, was a De Havilland Chipmunk coming in to land at White Waltham airfield.

4 March 1961

61 Just two days after Christmas and the last picture of the year. I have included my favourite piece of machinery No. 6000 **King George V** climbing Hatton Bank with the 09.10 Paddington-Birkenhead train. Do not be confused by the wheels being below rail level as the goods loop is unfortunately at a slightly higher level.

27 December 1960

63 The members' train going to Newbury Races was made up of first-class stock and always had an immaculate locomotive, usually a "King" class. In this case it is a double-chimney "Castle" No. 5056 **Earl of Powis** passing White Waltham complete with Great Western restaurant car.

4 March 1961

Wellington boots are very much the part of a railway photographer's equipment, although on this sunny spring day they were not required. D821 **Greyhound** flashes past on an up Weston-super-Mare express with the passenger in the third compartment fast asleep — probably because he was the only one with his window closed!

4 March 1961

64

65

The same location beside White Waltham airfield. No. 6019 **King Henry V** has 13 bogies in tow as it nears the end of its journey from Cardiff to Paddington with "The Red Dragon". This is another example of the small allocation of "King" class engines to Cardiff Canton for working the London trains.

4 March 1961

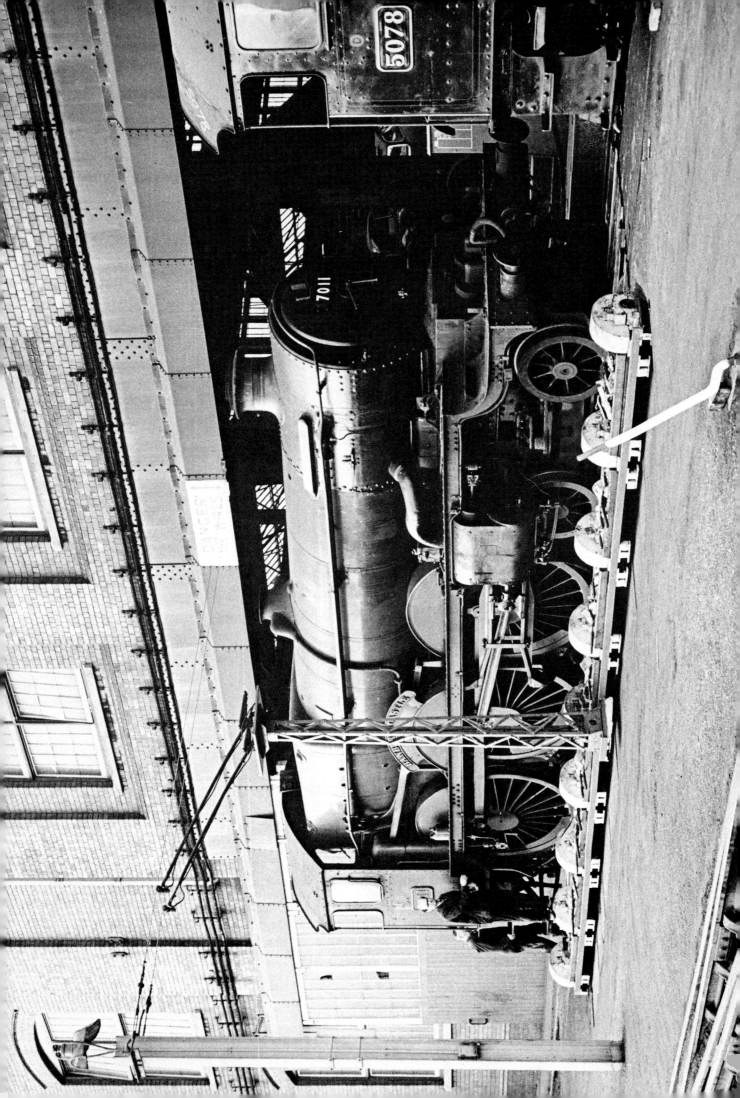

A shop at Swindon works after it had received its major overhaul. However, the next best was to see it in service as shown in picture No. 88. No. 5078 **Beaufort** is just visible with "Warship" diesels inside the works.

30 March 1961

outside the stock shed until work commenced on the restoration necessary for its presentation to the Science Museum in London.

This photograph clearly shows the enormous amount of work which was undertaken, the engine being completely stripped and sent out as new. The preservationists working at steam centres in this country today would envy the facilities available here.

30 March 1961

68 Through carriages and restaurant car from Newcastle to Bournemouth West headed by No. 7911 **Lady Margaret Hall** hurry through Beaulieu Road station in the New Forest.

This engine was shedded at Oxford and named after the ladies' college at the University. When my twin sister was up at Oxford, indeed at Lady Margaret Hall, she used to come home to Leamington behind this engine which always gave me

69 Most pictures taken during the afternoon in Harbury Cutting are from the sunny side. However, the shadow side is sometimes attractive and would have been more so had the engine been clean. No. 6022 **King Edward III** had worked up to London on the 09.35 Wolverhampton and is shown returning at speed on the 16.10 Paddington to Birkenhead.

22 July 1961

70 Shortly after Old Oak Common West Junction the Birmingham line passes under a bridge carrying a freight line from Acton to Willesden and the Midland at Cricklewood. No. 5090 **Neath Abbey** passes beneath this bridge with the 15.10 Paddington-Wolverhampton train which was always worked by an engine from 81A.
26 July 1961

71 Turning further round from the previous picture No. 6022 **King Edward III** is seen accelerating the 16.10 Paddington-Birkenhead away from Old Oak Common.

The line in the foreground, long since removed, used to carry trains from the Great Western Railway down through Olympia and to the Southern Railway.
26 July 1961

72   When I took this picture I did not realise that No. 4086 **Builth Castle** would be withdrawn early the following year but I did assume the writing was on the wall for all the class. In this scene a through working of Southern stock passes Leamington Spa South Junction signal box on its way north with returning holidaymakers. The significance of the broken cars is quite obvious.

5 August 1961

73 In human terms these two must have been exchanging pleasantries. Indeed, it makes one wonder if the driver of No. 6025 **King Henry III** intentionally pulled up early so that they could converse! The 09.10 Paddington-Birkenhead train is at Leamington Spa General with a d.m.u. waiting in the bay to proceed to Stratford-upon-Avon.

74 "Hall" class engines were very unusual on the up "Cambrian Coast Express" as it was very much the domain of the "Kings". Deputizing for a failure No. 4947 **Nanhoran Hall** from Bristol Bath Road shed climbs past Fosse Box and making some good black smoke from what looks like a load of indifferent coal in the tender.

75 Leamington shed may be seen at the top of the picture on the right and the Warnford Hospital stands out behind No. 6995 **Benthall Hall** as it approaches the station over a brick viaduct with an iron ore train from Banbury. The White Lion has since been demolished and the site is now an industrial complex.

29 August 1961

reached Princes Risborough.

Just minutes before the 09.10 Paddington-Birkenhead ran through the station the light appeared and No. 6024 **King Edward I** looked a magnificent sight as it swept by with a 12-wheel sleeping car leading the train. The d.m.u. in the bay platform will be for Oxford via Thame.

2 September 1961

77 Maybe this notice is still by the line above Princes Risborough station but it is a typical example of how to confuse simple sort of people like me. Although I do enjoy the wording the punch line is at the end and you may have to read it again to see if the moped you are riding qualifies!

2 September 1961

78 On the up line between Princes Risborough and Saunderton there is a short tunnel which No. 6007 **King William III** has just left and is seen here continuing the climb at 1 in 167 to the summit of the Chiltern Hills.

The train is the 11.35 Wolverhampton-Paddington with a Hawkesworth coach, probably built just after Nationalization.

2 September 1961

79   A Sunday morning back at Old Oak Common shed with Driver George Green and his fireman Douglas Godden standing in front of No. 6000 **King George V** which they were taking out to Birmingham with a Sunday excursion.

24 September 1961

80 Out in the yard and No. 6000 **King George V** is slowly moving backwards on its way to Paddington station to pick up its train. Note the siding signal allowing the engine out of the yard.

24 September 1961

81 No. 5041 **Tiverton Castle** was shedded at Neath (87A) in South Wales and is being serviced at Old Oak Common prior to returning home. No. 1500 requires no comment. The picture says all that is necessary when comparing the two engines.

24 September 1961

82 How lucky to find this engine ex-works at Old Oak Common as today it is the only "Hall" class locomotive passed for main-line running. No. 6998 **Burton Agnes Hall** stands off the south-west turntable with a light covering of dust on the boiler barrel.

83 No. 6012 **King Edward VI** sparkles in a ray of sunshine where it has been stabled next to three B.R. Class 9 2-10-0 freight engines.
The letters ID painted on the footplate angle iron immediately behind the

24 September 1961

84 You will notice the way in which all the oil and grease has been burnt off the axle-box and axle due to the bearing running hot.

The wheel is the front nearside on the bogie of a "Castle" class locomotive and the picture taken in the repair shop gives an indication as to how dirt collects on the more inaccessible parts. Note the lubrication pipe protruding with its cork stopper.

24 September 1961

85 In the background loaded coal wagons are shunted up to the coal stage. On the left of the picture and in the foreground the tender of No. 7009 **Athelney Castle** has just been filled with water. The chain flies through the air as the pipe is swung

...Pullman". With a 16.50 departure No. 7033 **Hartlebury Castle** will have some fast running to reach Leamington, the first stop in 89 minutes.

The set of Pullman stock was kept at Old Oak Common in case one of the Diesel Pullman units should not be available for service.

25 September 1961

87 No. 7006 **Lydford Castle** has just backed onto its train and the fireman is jumping down to collect his lamp from the platform. With the clock in the background saying 17.00 there is plenty of time to get the engine prepared for the 17.15 departure to Worcester and Hereford.

25 September 1961

Ranelagh Yard for servicing before returning to Worcester in the afternoon.

The engine had worked up with the "Cathedrals Express" — the only titled train on the Worcester line.

26 September 1961

his face, after the last passenger to leave the 09.35 Wolverhampton-Paddington train turned to look at the engine as he left Platform No. 7.

The two photographs show the single and double chimney "Castles" and also which side of the station is best illuminated for photography.

26 September 1961

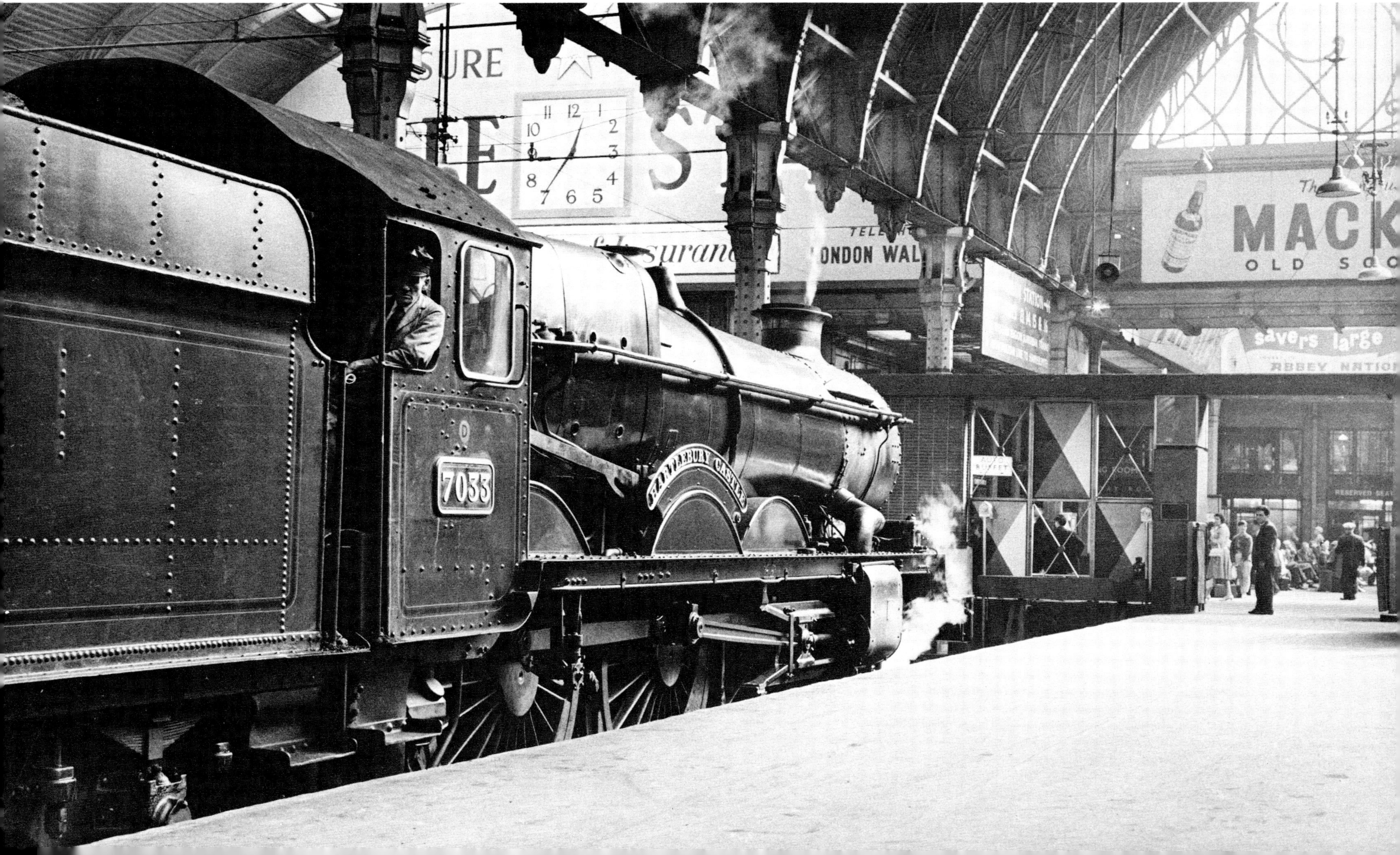

90 I must have been on holiday during the week this picture was taken. The time would be around 11.40 and No. 6029 **King Edward VIII** is passing Warwick station with the down 10.10 "Birmingham Pullman". Although the diesel electric "Blue Pullman" was fairly reliable, steam seemed a too regular substitute in the

91 2-8-0 No. 4704 runs into Shrewsbury with the "Talyllyn Railway Preservation Society Special" train from Paddington to Towyn. The elegant cast-iron chimney is clearly shown as well as an exemplary state of cleanliness.

Although specialist sources of information state that this engine had sniffing valves on the outside of the steam chests, at this stage in its life they must have

93 How fortunate that this section of the Cambrian line has been saved, running as it does along the north shore of the River Dovey.

2-6-2T No. 5555 and Collett 0-6-0 No. 2222 are nearing the end of their journey from Shrewsbury to Towyn and passing Panteidal near Aberdovey.

30 September 1961

---

from Shrewsbury and this caused the up "Cambrian Coast Express" headed by No. 7803 **Barcote Manor** to be stopped at Buttington Junction. The fireman has been down to the signal box obviously annoyed that in getting the fire in good shape for the climb ahead it is producing unwanted steam.

The siding went to a brick works across the main road and can you see the smoke from a set of thrashing tackle on the right of the picture?

30 September 1961

94 For a short time the up "Inter-City" was double-headed by a "Castle" and "King" or two "Castle" class locomotives. The sun is getting low in the sky at this time of the year and produces a dramatic lighting effect as No. 5089 **Westminster Abbey** and No. 6021 **King Richard II** leave Leamington Spa. The signal post, above the second coach, denuded of its arm, used to allow trains at the South Junction crossing to join the line from Leamington to Rugby.

6 October 1961

95 No. 6021 **King Richard II** starts away from Leamington Spa with the 14.35 Wolverhampton-Paddington train. The station is just out of the picture on the left and you will notice the enormous brick viaduct which is used by both the L.M.S. and G.W.R. lines.

One of the six largest parish churches in England, All Saints dominates the skyline at the south end of the town.

28 October 1961

96 Another view at Leamington Spa General station with No. 6008 **King James II** standing at the up platform with the 10.35 Wolverhampton-Paddington train.

The driver has been round the engine with an oil-can topping up the lubricators and Bert Smith starts down the train to tap the carriage wheels and check that all is in order.

28 October 1961

moment.

2-8-0 No. 48751 has backed into the up goods siding at Southam Road and Harbury station to enable No. 6005 **King George II** to pass by with the 11.35 Wolverhampton-Paddington train.

2 December 1961

98   Another dull day without any sign of sunshine but fortunately the front engine is making a worth-while smoke effect.

No. 6911 **Holker Hall** and No. 4082 **Windsor Castle** approach Hatton station with an overloaded 09.10 Paddington-Birkenhead train.

17 February 1962

99   Leaving Leamington Spa and into a hazy sunshine No. 6023 **King Edward II** accelerates the train shown in the adjoining photograph.

14 March 1962

100   This picture marked the beginning of the end for the "King" class so far as I was concerned. A dirty engine recently stabled at Stafford Road with a Cardiff Canton shed plate still in position. My favourite, No. 6006 **King George I**, had already been withdrawn in the preceding month and the complete class had disappeared before the end of the year.

In the first part of the morning at this time there were fast trains to London via Bicester leaving Leamington at 08.00, 08.08, 08.30 and 09.25. This picture shows the arrival of the 07.35 Wolverhampton-Paddington train at Leamington Spa, headed by No. 6023 **King Edward II**.

14 March 1962

101 I believe this engine, No. 6011 **King James I**, was the last of the Stafford Road "King" class to receive a major overhaul earlier in the year. In this picture it is climbing away from Leamington Spa on a 1 in 240 gradient. The train is the 08.33 Wolverhampton-Paddington which ran non-stop to London, but just compare the load with that carried today by the Brush Type 4 diesel-electrics.

102
103

Both these pictures were taken from Warwick goods yard and show the main line to Birmingham disappearing under the bridge in the background.

0-6-0PT No. 3619 (right) from Leamington shed has been put into the up Warwick goods loop to allow an express to pass. The signal is "off" for the 09.10 Paddington with No. 6021 **King Richard II** in charge.

In the lower photograph 0-6-0T No. 6604 in green livery shunts the yard — in this case petrol tank wagons for the storage terminal in the background.

Whilst not possessing the glamour of the express engines, the smaller engines shunting goods wagons to and fro was always a relaxing sight and if the approach was right a ride was often possible.

17 March 1962

104 Oxford shed has provided No. 5025 **Chirk Castle** as motive power for the 08.35 Bournemouth West to Wolverhampton complete with restaurant buffet and reserved seats if required at 2s 0d each.

The engine is picking up water on Lapworth troughs and why is the handrail

105 Where the location is suitable I often preferred the broadside picture and this one is particularly interesting as the crew are leaning out of the window, the fireman probably having been firing most of the way up to Harbury Cutting from Leamington. No. 6020 **King Henry IV** has the 11.35 Wolverhampton-Paddington train with a Hawksworth coach leading.

Here, No. 6027 **King Richard I** has the 17.10 down train to Wolverhampton and No. 7002 **Devizes Castle** the 17.15 "Cathedrals Express" to Worcester with through carriages to Hereford and Kidderminster. In Platform 2 an unidentified "Hall" class awaits departure with Platform 1 having just been vacated by No. 7034 **Ince Castle** with the "Cheltenham Spa Express". A scene full of activity and interest.

18 July 1962

Since I was travelling on the train hauled by No. 6027 **King Richard I** a compartment near the engine was always chosen and this picture was taken through the top sliding window. The driver is attending to the motion, and the reversing handwheel and speedometer are clearly shown.

In the background a "Hall" class engine moves into a platform underneath Bishops Bridge Road.

18 July 1962

108 Now looking a little sorry for itself compared with picture No. 91 2-8-0 No. 4704 moves out of Banbury yard with a down freight. I had spotted this engine when crossing the bridge in the background and after a sprint up the track I was just in time to see it leave.

21 July 1962

109 At the north end of Banbury station No. 4961 **Pyrland Hall** awaits in the down bay while Class B1 No. 61028 **Umseke** is ready to leave for Woodford Halse with the 09.35 from Banbury.

Part of the new station is visible but today it is impossible to imagine the size of the railway operation which once was carried out non-stop throughout the 24 hours in the marshalling yards and locomotive depot.

21 July 1962

110 This can only be Reading station looking west with No. 5032 **Usk Castle** preparing to leave with the 09.15 Paddington to Hereford. I had travelled down from London to stay at Reading awhile to see the Newbury Race specials pass through behind No. 6000 and No. 6002. This was a sad occasion as they were all polished to perfection and it was the last time I ever saw a "King" class engine in service except for the odd special working.

14 September 1962

111

Walking up the central island platform at Reading gave one a sense of anticipation to see what was acting as the east end station pilot. Ready with express headlamps fitted, in case of a diesel failure, is No. 5979 **Cruckton Hall.**

At the west end of the station on similar duties could be found on the same day in spotless condition No. 5018 **St. Mawes Castle.**

14 September 1962

Since it was such a fine autumn day I decided to travel home to Leamington by diesel multiple unit and sat in the front seat behind the driver's compartment.

We were just pulling away from Radley when an up Worcester express came through the station behind No. 4089 **Donnington Castle.** Needless to say I had been waiting for it with Leica at the ready — a situation where the small 35 mm camera is always the best instrument.

14 September 1962

After developing a roll of film I was going to ... to check for sharpness and blemishes. It was only after printing this picture that I realized the sinister shape above the safety valve bonnet of No. 1013 **County of Dorset** was a double-arm siding signal and not an imperfection on the negative.

The freight train is accelerating down the gradient and away from Ruabon station.

29 September 1962

... ... in September was allowed to a pilgrimage to see No. 6000 **King George V** arrive at Ruabon with the Talyllyn Railway Special train from London.

While waiting for the special train I saw No. 6928 **Underley Hall** come through the station with an up freight watched by engine spotters of the period.

29 September 1962

115 Turning round from the previous picture is the sight for which I had been waiting — the impeccably turned out engine just as it is today in preservation at H.P. Bulmers, Hereford. It must have taken many hours of preparation to look like this but the sight gave so much pleasure to admirers of the "King" class as most of them were inactive by this time.

Here, No. 6000 **King George V** has just shut off steam for the end of its journey at Ruabon.

29 September 1962.

116 Under a threatening sky No. 7814 **Fringford Manor** brings a down train through the outskirts of Shrewsbury.

The first coach has the middle compartment removed allowing an automatic self-service buffet to be installed open to the corridor. This auto buffet dispensing snacks, soft drinks, confectionary and cigarettes was being tested instead of a restaurant buffet on the "Cambrian Coast Express" between Aberystwyth and Shrewsbury.

117
118

Shrewsbury shed again with No. 7823 **Hook Norton Manor** being prepared for work and standing by the coal stage. In the afternoon No. 6000 **King George V** had run light engine to Shrewsbury shed for servicing and I had already taken many pictures when I came upon the tail lamp mounted on the tender.

This detail shows the affection bestowed on this engine with the white-painted lamp body and engine number on the side. Of more interest is the brass plate above the lamp glass which is simply engraved "King George V".

29 September 1962

119

Study this picture. The "Warship" diesel hydraulic conveying through carriages from Glasgow and Liverpool to Plymouth is totally unloved. No one looks at it and indeed all the class have now been withdrawn. The schoolboy admiration for the steam engine survives and the scene could almost be a "Return to Steam" run of 1975. This picture shows No. 6000 **King George V** about to leave Shrewsbury station on the 17.10 to Wolverhampton stopping at all stations.

29 September 1962

120 There seems little to say about these two pictures. The boy above takes his turn at ringing the
121 bell and in the cab the rest of the throng queue up for the driver's autograph with one client
obviously very satisfied.

29 September 1962